Parallel Programming with Python

Develop efficient parallel systems using the robust Python environment

Jan Palach

BIRMINGHAM - MUMBAI

Parallel Programming with Python

First published: June 2014

Production reference: 1180614

Published by Packt Publishing Ltd.
Livery Place
35 Livery Street
Birmingham B3 2PB, UK.

ISBN 978-1-78328-839-7

www.packtpub.com

Cover image by Lis Marie Martini (lismmartini@hotmail.com)

Credits

Author
Jan Palach

Reviewers
Cyrus Dasadia
Wei Di
Michael Galloy
Ludovic Gasc
Kamran Hussain
Bruno Torres

Commissioning Editor
Rebecca Youé

Acquisition Editor
Llewellyn Rozario

Content Development Editor
Sankalp Pawar

Technical Editors
Novina Kewalramani
Humera Shaikh

Copy Editors
Roshni Banerjee
Sarang Chari
Gladson Monteiro

Project Coordinator
Lima Danti

Proofreaders
Simran Bhogal
Maria Gould
Paul Hindle

Indexers
Mehreen Deshmukh
Rekha Nair
Tejal Soni
Priya Subramani

Graphics
Disha Haria
Abhinash Sahu

Production Coordinator
Saiprasad Kadam

Cover Work
Saiprasad Kadam

About the Author

Jan Palach has been a software developer for 13 years, having worked with scientific visualization and backend for private companies using C++, Java, and Python technologies. Jan has a degree in Information Systems from Estácio de Sá University, Rio de Janeiro, Brazil, and a postgraduate degree in Software Development from Paraná State Federal Technological University. Currently, he works as a senior system analyst at a private company within the telecommunication sector implementing C++ systems; however, he likes to have fun experimenting with Python and Erlang—his two technological passions. Naturally curious, he loves challenges and learning new technologies, meeting new people, and learning about different cultures.

Acknowledgments

I had no idea how hard it could be to write a book with such a tight deadline among so many other things taking place in my life. I had to fit the writing into my routine, taking care of my family, karate lessons, work, Diablo III, and so on. The task was not easy; however, I got to the end of it hoping that I have generated quality content to please most readers, considering that I have focused on the most important thing based on my experience.

The list of people I would like to acknowledge is so long that I would need a book only for this. So, I would like to thank some people I have constant contact with and who, in a direct or indirect way, helped me throughout this quest.

My wife Anicieli Valeska de Miranda Pertile, the woman I chose to share my love with and gather toothbrushes with to the end of this life, who allowed me to have the time to create this book and did not let me give up when I thought I could not make it. My family has always been important to me during my growth as a human being and taught me the path of goodness.

I would like to thank Fanthiane Ketrin Wentz, who beyond being my best friend is also guiding me through the ways of martial arts, teaching me the values I will carry during a lifetime—a role model for me. Lis Marie Martini, dear friend who provided the cover for this book, and who is an incredible photographer and animal lover.

Big thanks to my former English teacher, reviser, and proofreader, Marina Melo, who helped along the writing of this book. Thanks to the reviewers and personal friends, Vitor Mazzi and Bruno Torres, who contributed a lot to my professional growth and still do.

Special thanks to Rodrigo Cacilhas, Bruno Bemfica, Rodrigo Delduca, Luiz Shigunov, Bruno Almeida Santos, Paulo Tesch (corujito), Luciano Palma, Felipe Cruz, and other people with whom I often talk to about technology. A special thanks to Turma B.

Big thanks to Guido Van Rossum for creating Python, which transformed programming into something pleasant; we need more of this stuff and less set/get.

About the Reviewers

Cyrus Dasadia has worked as a Linux system administrator for over a decade for organizations such as AOL and InMobi. He is currently developing CitoEngine, an open source alert management service written entirely in Python.

Wei Di is a research scientist at eBay Research Labs, focusing on advanced computer vision, data mining, and information retrieval technologies for large-scale e-commerce applications. Her interest covers large-scale data mining, machine learning in merchandising, data quality for e-commerce, search relevance, and ranking and recommender systems. She also has years of research experience in pattern recognition and image processing. She received her PhD from Purdue University in 2011 with focuses on data mining and image classification.

Michael Galloy works as a research mathematician for Tech-X Corporation involved in scientific visualizations using IDL and Python. Before that, he worked for five years teaching all levels of IDL programming and consulting for Research Systems, Inc. (now Exelis Visual Information Solutions). He is the author of Modern IDL (`modernidl.idldev.com`) and is the creator/maintainer of several open source projects, including IDLdoc, mgunit, dist_tools, and cmdline_tools. He has written over 300 articles on IDL, scientific visualization, and high-performance computing for his website `michaelgalloy.com`. He is the principal investigator for NASA grants *Remote Data Exploration with IDL* for DAP bindings in IDL and *A Rapid Model Fitting Tool Suite* for accelerating curve fitting using modern graphic cards.

Ludovic Gasc is a senior software integration engineer at Eyepea, a highly renowned open source VoIP and unified communications company in Europe. Over the last five years, Ludovic has developed redundant distributed systems for Telecom based on Python (Twisted and now AsyncIO) and RabbitMQ.

He is also a contributor to several Python libraries. For more information and details on this, refer to `https://github.com/GMLudo`.

Kamran Husain has been in the computing industry for about 25 years, programming, designing, and developing software for the telecommunication and petroleum industry. He likes to dabble in cartooning in his free time.

Bruno Torres has worked for more than a decade, solving a variety of computing problems in a number of areas, touching a mix of client-side and server-side applications. Bruno has a degree in Computer Science from Universidade Federal Fluminense, Rio de Janeiro, Brazil.

Having worked with data processing, telecommunications systems, as well as app development and media streaming, he developed many different skills starting from Java and C++ data processing systems, coming through solving scalability problems in the telecommunications industry and simplifying large applications customization using Lua, to developing apps for mobile devices and supporting systems.

Currently he works at a large media company, developing a number of solutions for delivering videos through the Internet for both desktop browsers and mobile devices.

He has a passion for learning different technologies and languages, meeting people, and loves the challenges of solving computing problems.

www.PacktPub.com

Support files, eBooks, discount offers, and more

You might want to visit www.PacktPub.com for support files and downloads related to your book.

Did you know that Packt offers eBook versions of every book published, with PDF and ePub files available? You can upgrade to the eBook version at www.PacktPub.com and as a print book customer, you are entitled to a discount on the eBook copy. Get in touch with us at service@packtpub.com for more details.

At www.PacktPub.com, you can also read a collection of free technical articles, sign up for a range of free newsletters and receive exclusive discounts and offers on Packt books and eBooks.

http://PacktLib.PacktPub.com

Do you need instant solutions to your IT questions? PacktLib is Packt's online digital book library. Here, you can access, read and search across Packt's entire library of books.

Why subscribe?

- Fully searchable across every book published by Packt
- Copy and paste, print and bookmark content
- On demand and accessible via web browser

Free access for Packt account holders

If you have an account with Packt at www.PacktPub.com, you can use this to access PacktLib today and view nine entirely free books. Simply use your login credentials for immediate access.

I dedicate this book in the loving memory of Carlos Farias Ouro de Carvalho Neto.

–Jan Palach

Table of Contents

Preface

Months ago, in 2013, I was contacted by Packt Publishing professionals with the mission of writing a book about parallel programming using the Python language. I had never thought of writing a book before and had no idea of the work that was about to come; how complex it would be to conceive this piece of work and how it would feel to fit it into my work schedule within my current job. Although I thought about the idea for over a couple of days, I ended up accepting the mission and said to myself that it will be a great deal of personal learning and a perfect chance to disseminate my knowledge of Python to a worldwide audience, and thus, hopefully leave a worthy legacy along my journey in this life.

The first part of this work is to outline its topics. It is not easy to please everybody; however, I believe I have achieved a good balance in the topics proposed in this mini book, in which I intended to introduce Python parallel programming combining theory and practice. I have taken a risk in this work. I have used a new format to show how problems can be solved, in which examples are defined in the first chapters and then solved by using the tools presented along the length of the book. I think this is an interesting format as it allows the reader to analyze and question the different modules that Python offers.

All chapters combine a bit of theory, thereby building the context that will provide you with some basic knowledge to follow the practical bits of the text. I truly hope this book will be useful for those adventuring into the world of Python parallel programming, for I have tried to focus on quality writing.

What this book covers

Chapter 1, Contextualizing Parallel, Concurrent, and Distributed Programming, covers the concepts, advantages, disadvantages, and implications of parallel programming models. In addition, this chapter exposes some Python libraries to implement parallel solutions.

Chapter 2, Designing Parallel Algorithms, introduces a discussion about some techniques to design parallel algorithms.

Chapter 3, Identifying a Parallelizable Problem, introduces some examples of problems, and analyzes if these problems can be divided into parallel pieces.

Chapter 4, Using the threading and concurrent.futures Modules, explains how to implement each problem presented in *Chapter 3, Identifying a Parallelizable Problem,* using the threading and concurrent.futures modules.

Chapter 5, Using Multiprocessing and ProcessPoolExecutor, covers how to implement each problem presented in *Chapter 3, Identifying a Parallelizable Problem,* using multiprocessing and ProcessPoolExecutor.

Chapter 6, Utilizing Parallel Python, covers how to implement each problem presented in *Chapter 3, Identifying a Parallelizable Problem,* using the parallel Python module.

Chapter 7, Distributing Tasks with Celery, explains how to implement each problem presented in *Chapter 3, Identifying a Parallelizable Problem,* using the Celery distributed task queue.

Chapter 8, Doing Things Asynchronously, explains how to use the asyncio module and concepts about asynchronous programming.

What you need for this book

Previous knowledge of Python programming is necessary as a Python tutorial will not be included in this book. Knowledge of concurrence and parallel programming is welcome since this book is designed for developers who are getting started in this category of software development. In regards to software, it is necessary to obtain the following:

- Python 3.3 and Python 3.4 (still under development) are required for *Chapter 8, Doing Things Asynchronously*
- Any code editor of the reader's choice is required
- Parallel Python module 1.6.4 should be installed

- Celery framework 3.1 is required for *Chapter 5, Using Multiprocessing and ProcessPoolExecutor*

- Any operating system of the reader's choice is required

Who this book is for

This book is a compact discussion about parallel programming using Python. It provides tools for beginner and intermediate Python developers. This book is for those who are willing to get a general view of developing parallel/concurrent software using Python, and to learn different Python alternatives. By the end of this book, you will have enlarged your toolbox with the information presented in the chapters.

Conventions

In this book, you will find a number of styles of text that distinguish between different kinds of information. Here are some examples of these styles, and an explanation of their meaning.

Code words in text are shown as follows: "In order to exemplify the use of the `multiprocessing.Pipe` object, we will implement a Python program that creates two processes, A and B."

A block of code is set as follows:

```
def producer_task(conn):
    value = random.randint(1, 10)
    conn.send(value)
    print('Value [%d] sent by PID [%d]' % (value, os.getpid()))
    conn.close()
```

Any command-line input or output is written as follows:

```
$celery -A tasks -Q sqrt_queue,fibo_queue,webcrawler_queue worker
--loglevel=info
```

 Warnings or important notes appear in a box like this.

 Tips and tricks appear like this.

Reader feedback

Feedback from our readers is always welcome. Let us know what you think about this book—what you liked or may have disliked. Reader feedback is important for us to develop titles that you really get the most out of.

To send us general feedback, simply send an e-mail to feedback@packtpub.com, and mention the book title via the subject of your message.

If there is a topic that you have expertise in and you are interested in either writing or contributing to a book, see our author guide on www.packtpub.com/authors.

Customer support

Now that you are the proud owner of a Packt book, we have a number of things to help you to get the most from your purchase.

Downloading the example code

You can download the example code files for all Packt books you have purchased from your account at http://www.packtpub.com. If you purchased this book elsewhere, you can visit http://www.packtpub.com/support and register to have the files e-mailed directly to you.

Errata

Although we have taken every care to ensure the accuracy of our content, mistakes do happen. If you find a mistake in one of our books—maybe a mistake in the text or the code—we would be grateful if you would report this to us. By doing so, you can save other readers from frustration and help us improve subsequent versions of this book. If you find any errata, please report them by visiting http://www.packtpub.com/submit-errata, selecting your book, clicking on the **errata submission form** link, and entering the details of your errata. Once your errata are verified, your submission will be accepted and the errata will be uploaded on our website, or added to any list of existing errata, under the Errata section of that title. Any existing errata can be viewed by selecting your title from http://www.packtpub.com/support.

Piracy

Piracy of copyright material on the Internet is an ongoing problem across all media. At Packt, we take the protection of our copyright and licenses very seriously. If you come across any illegal copies of our works, in any form, on the Internet, please provide us with the location address or website name immediately so that we can pursue a remedy.

Please contact us at `copyright@packtpub.com` with a link to the suspected pirated material.

We appreciate your help in protecting our authors, and our ability to bring you valuable content.

Questions

You can contact us at `questions@packtpub.com` if you are having a problem with any aspect of the book, and we will do our best to address it.

1
Contextualizing Parallel, Concurrent, and Distributed Programming

Parallel programming can be defined as a model that aims to create programs that are compatible with environments prepared to execute code instructions simultaneously. It has not been too long since techniques of parallelism began to be used to develop software. Some years ago, processors had a single **Arithmetic Logic Unit (ALU)** among other components, which could only execute one instruction at a time during a time space. For years, only a clock that measured in hertz to determine the number of instructions a processor could process within a given interval of time was taken into consideration. The more the number of clocks, the more the instructions potentially executed in terms of KHz (thousands of operations per second), MHz (millions of operations per second), and the current GHz (billions of operations per second).

Summing up, the more instructions per cycle given to the processor, the faster the execution. During the '80s, a revolutionary processor came to life, *Intel 80386*, which allowed the execution of tasks in a pre-emptive manner, that is, it was possible to periodically interrupt the execution of a program to provide processor time to another program; this meant pseudo-parallelism based on *time-slicing*.

In the late '80s, there came *Intel 80486* that implemented a *pipelining system*, which in practice, divided the stage of execution into distinct substages. In practical terms, in a cycle of the processor, we could have different instructions being carried out simultaneously in each substage.

All the advances mentioned in the preceding section resulted in several improvements in performance, but it was not enough, as we were faced with a delicate issue that would end up as the so-called *Moore's law* (http://www.mooreslaw.org/).

The quest for high taxes of clock ended up colliding with physical limitations; processors would consume more energy, thereby generating more heat. Moreover, there was another as important issue: the market for portable computers was speeding up in the '90s. So, it was extremely important to have processors that could make the batteries of these pieces of equipment last long enough away from the plug. Several technologies and families of processors from different manufacturers were born. As regards servers and mainframes, Intel® deserves to be highlighted with its family of products Core®, which allowed to trick the operating system by simulating the existence of more than one processor even though there was a single physical chip.

In the Core® family, the processor got severe internal changes and featured components called **core**, which had their own ALU and caches *L2* and *L3*, among other elements to carry out instructions. Those cores, also known as **logical processors**, allowed us to parallel the execution of different parts of the same program, or even different programs, simultaneously. The age core enabled lower energy use with power processing superior to its predecessors. As cores work in parallel, simulating independent processors, we can have a *multi-core* chip and an inferior clock, thereby getting superior performance compared to a single-core chip with higher clock, depending on the task.

So much evolution has, of course, changed the way we approach software designing. Today, we must think of parallelism to design systems that make rational use of resources without wasting them, thereby providing a better experience to the user and saving energy not only in personal computers, but also at processing centers. More than ever, parallel programming is in the developers' daily lives and, apparently, it will never go back.

This chapter covers the following topics:

- Why use parallel programming?
- Introducing the common forms of parallelization
- Communicating in parallel programming
- Identifying parallel programming problems
- Discovering Python's programming tools
- Taking care of Python **Global Interpreter Lock (GIL)**

Why use parallel programming?

Since computing systems have evolved, they have started to provide mechanisms that allow us to run independent pieces of a specific program in parallel with one another, thus enhancing the response and the general performance. Moreover, we can easily verify that the machines are equipped with more processors and these with plenty of more cores. So, why not take advantage of this architecture?

Parallel programming is a reality in all contexts of system development, from smart phones and tablets, to heavy duty computing in research centers. A solid basis in parallel programming will allow a developer to optimize the performance of an application. This results in enhancement of user experience as well as consumption of computing resources, thereby taking up less processing time for the accomplishment of complex tasks.

As an example of parallelism, let us picture a scenario in which an application that, amongst other tasks, selects information from a database, and this database has considerable size. Consider as well, the application being sequential, in which tasks must be run one after another in a logical sequence. When a user requests data, the rest of the system will be blocked until the data return is not concluded. However, making use of parallel programming, we will be allowed to create a new worker that which will seek information in this database without blocking other functions in the application, thus enhancing its use.

Exploring common forms of parallelization

There is a certain confusion when we try to define the main forms of paralleling systems. It is common to find quotations on parallel and concurrent systems as if both meant the same thing. Nevertheless, there are slight differences between them.

Within concurrent programming, we have a scenario in which a program dispatches several workers and these workers dispute to use the CPU to run a task. The stage at which the dispute takes place is controlled by the *CPU scheduler*, whose function is to define which worker is apt for using the resource at a specific moment. In most cases, the CPU scheduler runs the task of raking processes so fast that we might get the impression of *pseudo-parallelism*. Therefore, concurrent programming is an abstraction from parallel programming.

 Concurrent systems dispute over the same CPU to run tasks.

The following diagram shows a concurrent program scheme:

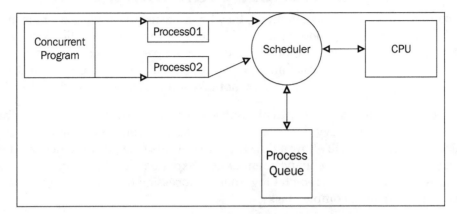

Concurrent programming scheme.

Parallel programming can be defined as an approach in which program data creates workers to run specific tasks simultaneously in a *multicore environment* without the need for concurrency amongst them to access a *CPU*.

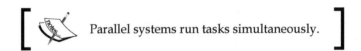 Parallel systems run tasks simultaneously.

The following figure shows the concept of parallel systems:

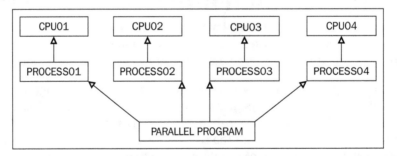

Parallel programming scheme.

Distributed programming aims at the possibility of sharing the processing by exchanging data through messages between machines (nodes) of computing, which are physically separated.

Distributed programming is becoming more and more popular for many reasons; they are explored as follows:

- **Fault-tolerance**: As the system is decentralized, we can distribute the processing to different machines in a network, and thus perform individual maintenance of specific machines without affecting the functioning of the system as a whole.

- **Horizontal scalability**: We can increase the capacity of processing in distributed systems in general. We can link new equipment with no need to abort applications being executed. We can say that it is cheaper and simpler compared to vertical scalability.

- **Cloud computing**: With the reduction in hardware costs, we need the growth of this type of business where we can obtaining huge machine parks acting in a cooperative way and running programs in a transparent way for their users.

[Distributed systems run tasks within physically-separated nodes.]

The following figure shows a distributed system scheme:

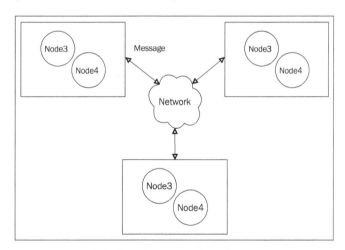

Distributed programming scheme.

Communicating in parallel programming

In parallel programming, the workers that are sent to perform a task often need to establish communication so that there can be cooperation in tackling a problem. In most cases, this communication is established in such a way that data can be exchanged amongst workers. There are two forms of communication that are more widely known when it comes to parallel programming: shared state and message passing. In the following sections, a brief description of both will be presented.

Understanding shared state

One the most well-known forms of communication amongst workers is *shared state*. Shared state seems straightforward to use but has many pitfalls because an invalid operation made to the shared resource by one of the processes will affect all of the others, thereby producing bad results. It also makes it impossible for the program to be distributed between multiple machines for obvious reasons.

Illustrating this, we will make use of a real-world case. Suppose you are a customer of a specific bank, and this bank has only one cashier. When you go to the bank, you must head to a queue and wait for your chance. Once in the queue, you notice that only one customer can make use of the cashier at a time, and it would be impossible for the cashier to attend two customers simultaneously without potentially making errors. Computing provides means to access data in a controlled way, and there are several techniques, such as *mutex*.

Mutex can be understood as a special process variable that indicates the level of availability to access data. That is, in our real-life example, the customer has a number, and at a specific moment, this number will be activated and the cashier will be available for this customer exclusively. At the end of the process, this customer will free the cashier for the next customer, and so on.

There are cases in which data has a constant value in a variable while the program is running, and the data is shared only for reading purposes. So, access control is not necessary because it will never present integrity problems.

Understanding message passing

Message passing is used when we aim to avoid data access control and synchronizing problems originating from shared state. Message passing consists of a mechanism for message exchange in running processes. It is very commonly used whenever we are developing programs with distributed architecture, where the message exchanges within the network they are placed are necessary. Languages such as *Erlang*, for instance, use this model to implement communication in its parallel architecture. Once data is copied at each message exchange, it is impossible that problems occur in terms of concurrence of access. Although memory use seems to be higher than in shared memory state, there are advantages to the use of this model. They are as follows:

- Absence of data access concurrence
- Messages can be exchange locally (various processes) or in distributed environments

- This makes it less likely that scalability issues occur and enables interoperability of different systems
- In general, it is easy to maintain according to programmers

Identifying parallel programming problems

There are classic problems that brave keyboard warriors can face while battling in the lands where parallel programming ghosts dwell. Many of these problems occur more often when inexperienced programmers make use of workers combined with shared state. Some of these issues will be described in the following sections.

Deadlock

Deadlock is a situation in which two or more workers keep indefinitely waiting for the freeing of a resource, which is blocked by a worker of the same group for some reason. For a better understanding, we will use another real-life case. Imagine the bank whose entrance has a rotating door. Customer A heads to the side, which will allow him to enter the bank, while customer B tries to exit the bank by using the entrance side of this rotating door so that both customers would be stuck forcing the door but heading nowhere. This situation would be hilarious in real life but tragic in programming.

 Deadlock is a phenomenon in which processes wait for a condition to free their tasks, but this condition will never occur.

Starvation

This is the issue whose side effects are caused by unfair raking of one or more processes that take much more time to run a task. Imagine a group of processes, A, which runs heavy tasks and has data processor priority. Now, imagine that a process A with high priority constantly consumes the CPU, while a lower priority process B never gets the chance. Hence, one can say that process B is *starving* for CPU cycles.

 Starvation is caused by badly adjusted policies of process ranking.

Race conditions

When the result of a process depends on a sequence of facts, and this sequence is broken due to the lack of synchronizing mechanisms, we face race conditions. They result from problems that are extremely difficult to filter in larger systems. For instance, a couple has a joint account; the initial balance before operations is $100. The following table shows the regular case, in which there are mechanisms of protection and the sequence of expected facts, as well as the result:

Husband	Wife	Account balance (dollars)
		100
Read balance		100
Adds 20		100
Concludes operation		120
	Read balance	120
	Withdraws 10	120
	Concludes operation	110

Presents baking operations without the chance of race conditions occurrence

In the following table, the problematic scenario is presented. Suppose that the account does not have mechanisms of synchronization and the order of operations is not as expected.

Husband	Wife	Account balance (dollars)
		100
Read balance		100
Withdraws 100		100
	Reads balance	100
	Withdraws 10	100
Concludes operation updating balance		0
	Concludes operation updating balance	90

Analogy to balance the problem in a joint account and race conditions

There is a noticeable inconsistency in the final result due to the unexpected lack of synchronization in the operations sequence. One of the parallel programming characteristics is *non-determinism*. It is impossible to foresee the moment at which two workers will be running, or even which of them will run first. Therefore, synchronization mechanisms are essential.

Non-determinism, if combined with lack of synchronization mechanisms, may lead to race condition issues.

Discovering Python's parallel programming tools

The *Python* language, created by Guido Van Rossum, is a multi-paradigm, multi-purpose language. It has been widely accepted worldwide due to its powerful simplicity and easy maintenance. It is also known as the language that has batteries included. There is a wide range of modules to make its use smoother. Within parallel programming, Python has built-in and external modules that simplify implementation. This work is based on Python 3.x.

The Python threading module

The Python *threading* module offers a layer of abstraction to the module _thread, which is a lower-level module. It provides functions that help the programmer during the hard task of developing parallel systems based on threads. The threading module's official papers can be found at `http://docs.python.org/3/library/threading.html?highlight=threading#module-threadin`.

The Python multiprocessing module

The *multiprocessing* module aims at providing a simple API for the use of parallelism based on processes. This module is similar to the threading module, which simplifies alternations between the processes without major difficulties. The approach that is based on processes is very popular within the Python users' community as it is an alternative to answering questions on the use of *CPU-Bound threads* and *GIL* present in Python. The multiprocessing module's official papers can be found at `http://docs.python.org/3/library/multiprocessing.html?highlight=multiprocessing#multiprocessing`.

The parallel Python module

The *parallel Python* module is external and offers a rich API for the creation of parallel and distributed systems making use of the processes approach. This module promises to be light and easy to install, and integrates with other Python programs. The parallel Python module can be found at `http://parallelpython.com`. Among some of the features, we may highlight the following:

- Automatic detection of the optimal configuration
- The fact that a number of worker processes can be changed during runtime
- Dynamic load balance
- Fault tolerance
- Auto-discovery of computational resources

Celery – a distributed task queue

Celery is an excellent Python module that's used to create distributed systems and has excellent documentation. It makes use of at least three different types of approach to run tasks in concurrent form—*multiprocessing*, *Eventlet*, and *Gevent*. This work will, however, concentrate efforts on the use of the multiprocessing approach. Also, the link between one and another is a configuration issue, and it remains as a study so that the reader is able to establish comparisons with his/her own experiments.

The Celery module can be obtained on the official project page at `http://celeryproject.org`.

Taking care of Python GIL

GIL is a mechanism that is used in implementing standard Python, known as **CPython**, to avoid *bytecodes* that are executed simultaneously by different threads. The existence of GIL in Python is a reason for fiery discussion amongst users of this language. GIL was chosen to protect the internal memory used by the CPython interpreter, which does not implement mechanisms of synchronization for the concurrent access by threads. In any case, GIL results in a problem when we decide to use threads, and these tend to be CPU-bound. *I/O Threads*, for example, are out of GIL's scope. Maybe the mechanism brings more benefits to the evolution of Python than harm to it. Evidently, we could not consider only *speed* as a single argument to determine whether something is good or not.

There are cases in which the approach to the use of processes for tasks sided with message passing brings better relations among maintainability, scalability, and performance. Even so, there are cases in which there will be a real need for threads, which would be subdued to GIL. In these cases, what could be done is write such pieces of code as extensions in *C language*, and embed them into the Python program. Thus, there are alternatives; it is up to the developer to analyze the real necessity. So, there comes the question: is GIL, in a general way, a villain? It is important to remember that, the *PyPy* team is working on an *STM* implementation in order to remove GIL from Python. For more details about the project, visit `http://pypy.org/tmdonate.html`.

Summary

In this chapter, we learned some parallel programming concepts, and learned about some models, their advantages, and disadvantages. Some of the problems and potential issues when thinking of parallelism have been presented in a brief explanations. We also had a short introduction to some Python modules, built-in and external, which makes a developer's life easier when building up parallel systems.

In the next chapter, we will be studying some techniques to design parallel algorithms.

2

Designing Parallel Algorithms

While developing parallel systems, several aspects must be observed before you start with the lines of code. Outlining the problem and the way it will be paralleled from the beginning are essential in order to obtain success along the task. In this chapter, we'll approach some technical aspects to achieve solutions.

This chapter covers the following topics:

- The divide and conquer technique
- Data decomposition
- Decomposing tasks with pipeline
- Processing and mapping

The divide and conquer technique

When you face a complex issue, the first thing to be done is to decompose the problem in order to identify parts of it that may be handled independently. In general, the parallelizable parts in a solution are in pieces that can be divided and distributed for them to be processed by different workers. The technique of dividing and conquering involves splitting the domain recursively until an indivisible unit of the complete issue is found and solved. The **sort** algorithms, such as **merge sort** and **quick sort**, can be resolved by using this approach.

The following diagram shows the application of a merge sort in a vector of six elements, making the divide and conquer technique visible:

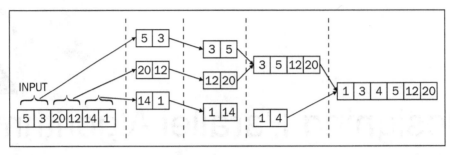

Merge sort (divide and conquer)

Using data decomposition

One of the ways to parallelize a problem is through data decomposition. Imagine a situation in which the task is to multiply a 2 x 2 matrix, which we will call **Matrix A**, by a scalar value of 4. In a sequential system, we will perform each multiplication operation one after the other, generating the final result at the end of all the instructions. Depending on the size of **Matrix A**, the sequential solution of the problem may be time consuming. However, when decomposition of data is applied, we can picture a scenario in which **Matrix A** is broken into pieces, and these pieces are associated with the workers that process the received data in a parallel way. The following diagram illustrates the concept of data decomposition applied to the example of a 2 x 2 matrix multiplied by a scalar value:

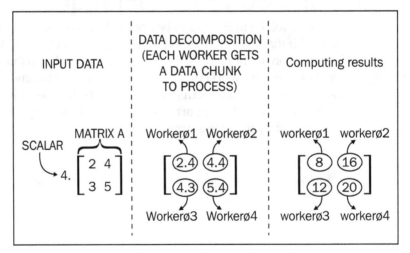

Data decomposition in a matrix example

The matrix problem presented in the preceding diagram had a certain symmetry where each necessary operation to get to the final result was executed by a single worker, and each worker executed the same number of operations to resolve the problem. Nevertheless, in real world, there is an asymmetry of the relation between the number of workers and the quantity of data that is decomposed, and this directly affects the performance of the solution. Finally, the results generated by each worker must be correlated in a way that the end of the program's output makes sense. In order to establish this correlation, workers must establish communication among them by means of using a message exchanging pattern or even a shared state standard.

 The granularity choice of data decomposition might affect the performance of a solution.

Decomposing tasks with pipeline

The pipeline technique is used to organize tasks that must be executed in a collaborative way to resolve a problem. Pipeline breaks large tasks into smaller independent tasks that run in a parallel manner. The pipeline model could be compared to an assembly line at a vehicle factory where the chassis is the raw material, the input. As the raw material goes through different stages of production, several workers perform different actions one after another until the end of the process so that we can have a car ready. This model is very similar to the sequential paradigm of development; tasks are executed on data one after another, and normally, a task gets an input, which is the result of the previous task. So what differentiates this model from the sequential technique? Each stage of the pipeline technique possesses its own workers that act in a parallel way on the problem.

An example in the context of computing could be one in which a system processes images in batches and persists data that is extracted into a database. We will have the following sequence of facts:

- Input images are received and lined in parallel to be processed at the second stage
- Images are parsed and useful information is sent to the third stage
- Filters are applied onto images in parallel during the third stage
- Data that results from the third stage is persisted in the database

 Each stage of the pipeline technique acts in an isolated way with its own workers. However, it establishes mechanisms of data communication so that there is an exchange of information.

The following diagram illustrates the pipeline concept:

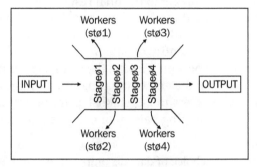

The pipeline technique

Processing and mapping

The number of workers is not always large enough to resolve a specific problem in a single step. Therefore, the decomposition techniques presented in the previous sections are necessary. However, decomposition techniques should not be applied arbitrarily; there are factors that can influence the performance of the solution. After decomposing data or tasks, the question we ought to ask is, "How do we divide the processing load among workers to obtain good performance?" This is not an easy question to answer, as it all depends on the problem under study.

Basically, we could mention two important steps when defining process mapping:

- Identifying independent tasks
- Identifying tasks that require data exchange

Identifying independent tasks

Identifying independent tasks in a system allows us to distribute the tasks among different workers, as these tasks do not need constant communication. As there is no need for a data location, tasks can be executed in different workers without impacting other task executions.

Identifying the tasks that require data exchange

Grouping the tasks that establish constant communication in a single worker can enhance the performance. This is true when there is a large load of data communication as it may help reduce the overhead in exchange of the information within the tasks.

Load balance

A relevant characteristic in a parallel solution is the way work units are distributed over different computing resources. The more we distribute tasks to different workers, the more we increase the granularity of the communication. On the other hand, the more tasks we group in a single worker, the more we reduce the overhead associated with communication. Still, we can increase idling, that is, idle computing power. Idleness is not nice in parallel programming. Moreover, the increase of location reduces the flexibility of the solution concerning the capacity to expand the computing power by simply adding up more equipment. Within an architecture based on messages (low data location), it is simple to add more machines to the cluster or grid, which increases its processing power without even interrupting the running of the system.

Summary

In this chapter, we discussed some ways to create parallel solutions. Your focus should be on the importance of dividing the processing load among different workers, considering the location and not the data.

In the next chapter, we will study how to identify a parallelizable problem.

3
Identifying a Parallelizable Problem

The previous chapter presented some of the different ways in which we can think about a problem in terms of parallelism. Now we will analyze some specific problems that will be useful in guiding us throughout the implementation.

This chapter covers the following topics:

- Obtaining the highest Fibonacci value for multiple inputs
- Crawling the Web

Obtaining the highest Fibonacci value for multiple inputs

It is known that the Fibonacci sequence is defined as follows:

$$F(n) = \begin{cases} 0, & if\ n = 0; \\ 1, & if\ n = 1; \\ F(n\text{-}1) + F(n\text{-}2) & if\ n > 1; \end{cases}$$

In practical terms, calculating the Fibonacci value for the terms 0 to 10, the result would be $0, 1, 1, 2, 3, 5, 8, 13, 21, 34$, and 55.

An example of Python code to calculate Fibonacci returning the highest value using the iterative method is as follows:

```
def fibonacci(input):
    a, b = 0, 1
    foritem in range(input):
        a, b = b, a + b
    return a
```

The Fibonacci function calculates the highest Fibonacci value for a specific piece of input data. Let us picture a hypothetical scenario in which it is necessary to calculate Fibonacci values, and this website will receive several inputs from a user. Suppose the user provides an array of values as input, so making these calculations sequentially would be interesting. But, what if 1 million users are connected at the same time to make requests? In this case, some users would have to wait for quite a long time until they are answered.

Let's think only within the context of the Python Fibonacci function presented in the preceding code. How could we draw it so as to make use of parallelism where there is an array of data input? The previous chapter displayed several techniques; we could use one of them in this case — data decomposition. We could decompose the array in units and dispatch a task associated with each unit to be executed by a worker. The following diagram depicts the suggested solution:

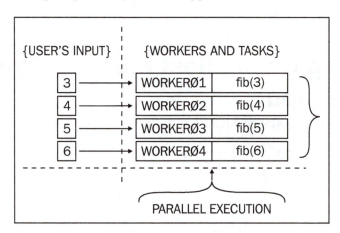

Parallel Fibonacci for multiples inputs.

 As a suggestion to the reader, complete the exercise of implementing the use of a mechanism to cache computed values in order to avoid wasting CPU time. We recommend something like memcached (http://memcached.org/).

Crawling the Web

Another problem to be studied throughout this book is the implementation of a parallel Web crawler. A **Web crawler** consists of a computer program that browses the Web to search for information on pages. The scenario to be analyzed is a problem in which a sequential Web crawler is fed by a variable number of **Uniform Resource Locators (URLs)**, and it has to search all the links within each URL provided. Imagining that the number of input URLs may be relatively large, we could plan a solution looking for parallelism in the following way:

1. Group all the input URLs in a data structure.

2. Associate data URLs with tasks that will execute the crawling by obtaining information from each URL.

3. Dispatch the tasks for execution in parallel workers.

4. The result from the previous stage must be passed to the next stage, which will improve raw collected data, thereby saving them and relating them to the original URLs.

As we can observe in the numbered steps for a proposed solution, there is a combination of the following two methods:

- **Data decomposition**: This occurs when we divide and associate URLs to tasks

- **Task decomposition with pipeline**: This contains a pipeline of three stages and occurs when we chain the task of receiving, collecting, and organizing the results of crawling

The following diagram shows the solution scheme:

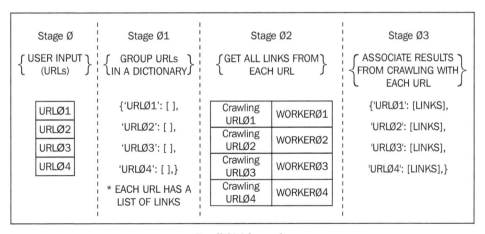

Parallel Web crawler

Summary

In this chapter, we learned about common problems and potential solutions involving parallelism. The problems presented will be shown using different parallel Python libraries for the implementation of solutions.

In the next chapter, we will focus on solutions involving threads while using the `threading` module, solutions involving the use of processes with the `multiprocessing` module, and so on.

4
Using the threading and concurrent.futures Modules

In the previous chapter, we presented some potential problems that may be solved with parallelism. In this chapter, we will analyze the implementation of the solutions of each problem using the `threading` module from the Python language.

This chapter covers the following topics:

- Defining threads
- Choosing between `threading` and `_thread`
- Using `threading` to obtain the Fibonacci series term for multiple inputs
- Crawling the Web using the `concurrent.futures` module

Defining threads

Threads are different execution lines in a process. Let us picture a program as if it was a hive, and there is a process of collecting pollen inside this hive. This collection process is carried out by several worker bees who work simultaneously in order to solve the problem of lack of pollen. The worker bees play the role of threads, acting inside a process and sharing resources to perform their tasks.

Threads belong to the same process and share the same memory space. Hence, the developer's task is to control and access these areas of memory.

Advantages and disadvantages of using threads

Some advantages and disadvantages have to be taken into account when deciding on the use of threads, and it depends on the language and operating system used to implement a solution.

The advantages of using threads are as follows:

- The speed of communication of the threads in the same process, data location, and shared information is fast

- The creation of threads is less costly than the creation of a process, as it is not necessary to copy all the information contained in the context of the main process

- Making the best use of data locality by optimizing memory access through the processor cache memory

The disadvantages of using threads are as follows:

- Data sharing allows swift communication. However, it also allows the introduction of difficult-to-solve errors by inexperienced developers.

- Data sharing limits the flexibility of the solution. Migrating to a distributed architecture, for instance, may cause a real headache. In general, they limit the scalability of algorithms.

 Within the Python programming language, the use of CPU-bound threads may harm performance of the application due to GIL.

Understanding different kinds of threads

There are two types of threads, kernel and user. The kernel threads are the threads that are created and managed by the operating system. The exchange of context, scheduling, and concluding are all managed by the kernel of the current operating system. For the user threads, these states are controlled by the package developer.

We can quote some advantages of each type of thread.

The advantages of the kernel threads are as follows:

- One kernel thread is referenced to one process. So if a kernel thread blocks, others can still run.

- The kernel threads can run on different CPUs.

The disadvantages of the kernel threads are as follows:

- The creation and synchronization routines are too expensive
- The implementation is platform dependent

The advantages of the user threads are as follows:

- The user thread has low cost for creation and synchronization
- The user thread is platform independent

The disadvantages of the user threads are as follows:

- All the user threads inside a process are related to only one kernel thread. So, if one user thread blocks, all the other user threads can't run.
- The user threads can't run on different CPUs.

Defining the states of a thread

There are five possible states in a thread's life span. They are as follows:

- **Creation**: This is the main process that creates a thread, and after its creation, it is sent to a line of threads ready for execution
- **Execution**: At this stage, the thread makes use of the CPU
- **Ready**: At this stage, the thread is in a line of threads ready for execution and bound to be executed
- **Blocked**: At this stage, the thread is blocked to wait for an I/O operation to happen, for example, and it does not make use of the CPU at this stage
- **Concluded**: At this stage, free resources are to be used in an execution and end the life span of the thread

Choosing between threading and _thread

The Python language offers two modules to support implementation for systems based on threads: the _thread module (this Python module offers an API of lower level for the use of threads; its documents can be found at http://docs.python. org/3.3/library/_thread.html) and the threading module (this Python module offers an API of higher level for the use of threads; its documents can be found at http://docs.python.org/3.3/library/threading.html). The threading module offers a friendly interface for the _thread module, making its use more convenient. The choice is up to the developer. If the developer finds it easy to use threads at a lower level, implementing their own thread pool and cuddling with locks and other primitive features, he/she would rather use _thread. Otherwise, threading is the most sensible choice.

Using threading to obtain the Fibonacci series term with multiple inputs

Now it is time for the truth. The mission is to parallelize the execution of the terms of the Fibonacci series when multiple input values are given. For didactical purposes, we will fix the input values in the four elements and the four threads to process each element, simulating a perfect symmetry among workers and tasks to be executed. The algorithm will work as follows:

1. First, a list will store the four values to be calculated and the values will be sent into a structure that allows synchronized access of threads.

2. After the values are sent to the synchronized structure, the threads that calculate the Fibonacci series need to be advised that the values are ready to be processed. For this, we will use a thread synchronization mechanism called Condition. (The Condition mechanism is one of the Python objects that offer data access synchronization mechanisms shared among threads; you can learn more at http://docs.python.org/3/library/threading. html#threading.Condition.)

3. After each thread finishes their Fibonacci series calculation, the results will be saved in a dictionary.

So, now we will present the code and comment on the interesting aspects.

At the beginning of the code, we have the additional support to Unicode and the import of the logging, threading, and Queue modules. In addition, we have defined the main data structures to be used in our example. A dictionary, which we will call fibo_dict, will store each integer (provided as an input) as a key, and its respective key values will be the Fibonacci series values calculated. We have also declared a Queue module present in the queue module, which will be the container of our shared data among threads that calculate the Fibonacci series and the thread that inserts elements in the Queue object. We will call this queue as shared_queue. Finally, we define the last data structure—a Python list object with four elements that simulates the set of values received by the program. The code is as follows:

```
#coding: utf-8

import logging, threading

from queue import Queue

logger = logging.getLogger()
logger.setLevel(logging.DEBUG)
formatter = logging.Formatter('%(asctime)s - %(message)s')

ch = logging.StreamHandler()
ch.setLevel(logging.DEBUG)
ch.setFormatter(formatter)
logger.addHandler(ch)

fibo_dict = {}
shared_queue = Queue()
input_list = [3, 10, 5, 7]
```

Downloading the example code

You can download the example code files for all Packt books you have purchased from your account at http://www.packtpub.com. If you purchased this book elsewhere, you can visit http://www.packtpub.com/support and register to have the files e-mailed directly to you.

In the following line of code, we will define an object from the threading module called Condition. This object aims to synchronize the access to resources according to a specific condition.

```
queue_condition = threading.Condition()
```

The idea of using the Condition object is to control the creation of a queue and the processing that takes place in it.

The next piece of code is a definition of the function to be executed by several threads. We will call it `fibonacci_task`. The `fibonacci_task` function receives the `condition` object as an argument that will control the `fibonacci_task` access to `shared_queue`. Inside the function, we made use of the `with` statement (for more information on the `with` statement, refer to `http://docs.python.org/3/reference/compound_stmts.html#with`) to simplify the managing of the content. Without the `with` statement, we would have to explicitly acquire the lock and release it. With the `with` statement, we can acquire the lock at the beginning and release it at the exit of the internal block. The following step in the `fibonacci_task` function is to make a logical evaluation, telling the current thread, "while `shared_queue` is empty, wait." This is the main use of the `wait()` method of the `condition` object. The thread will wait until it gets notified that `shared_queue` is free to process. Once we have the condition satisfied, the current thread will obtain an element in `shared_queue`, which right away calculates the Fibonacci series value and generates an entry in the `fibo_dict` dictionary. In the end, we make a call to the `task_done()` method, which aims to inform that a certain queued task has been extracted and executed. The code is as follows:

```python
def fibonacci_task(condition):
    with condition:
        while shared_queue.empty():
            logger.info("[%s] - waiting for elements in queue.."
                % threading.current_thread().name)
            condition.wait()
        else:
            value = shared_queue.get()
            a, b = 0, 1
            for item in range(value):
                a, b = b, a + b
                fibo_dict[value] = a
        shared_queue.task_done()
        logger.debug("[%s] fibonacci of key [%d] with
            result [%d]" %
            (threading.current_thread().name, value,
                fibo_dict[value]))
```

The second function that we defined is the `queue_task` function that will be executed by the thread responsible for populating `shared_queue` with elements to be processed. We can notice the acquisition of `condition` received as an argument to access `shared_queue`. For each item present in `input_list`, the thread inserts them in `shared_queue`.

After it inserts all the elements into `shared_queue`, the function notifies the threads responsible for calculating the Fibonacci series that the queue is ready to be used. This is done by using `condition.notifyAll()` as follows:

```
def queue_task(condition):
    logging.debug('Starting queue_task...')
    with condition:
        for item in input_list:
            shared_queue.put(item)
        logging.debug("Notifying fibonacci_task threads
            that the queue is ready to consume..")
        condition.notifyAll()
```

In the next piece of code, we created a set of four threads that will wait for the preparing condition from `shared_queue`. We then highlight the constructor of the `thread` class that allows us to define the function. The thread will execute using the `target` argument, and the arguments this function receives in `args` are as follows:

```
threads = [threading.Thread(
    daemon=True, target=fibonacci_task,
args=(queue_condition,)) for i in range(4)]
```

Then, we started the execution of the threads created to calculate the Fibonacci series by using the following code:

```
[thread.start() for thread in threads]
```

In the next step, we created a thread that will populate `shared_queue` and start its execution. The code is as follows:

```
prod = threading.Thread(name='queue_task_thread', daemon=True,
    target=queue_task, args=(queue_condition,))
prod.start()
```

And finally, we called the `join()` method to all the threads that calculate the Fibonacci series. The aim of this call is to make the `main` thread wait for the execution of the Fibonacci series from these threads so that it will not end the main flux of the program before the end of their process. Refer to the following code:

```
[thread.join() for thread in threads]
```

As a result of the execution of this program, we have the following output:

The parallel_fibonacci.py output

Notice that at first the `fibonacci_task` threads are created and initialized, and then they enter the waiting state. In the meantime, `queue_task` is created and populates `shared_queue`. In the end, `queue_task` notifies the `fibonacci_task` threads that they can execute their tasks.

Notice that the order in which the `fibonacci_task` threads execute does not follow a sequential logic, and the order may vary for each execution. This is a characteristic of the use of threads: non-determinism.

Crawling the Web using the concurrent. futures module

The following section will make use of our code by implementing the parallel Web crawler. In this scheme, we will use a very interesting Python resource, `ThreadPoolExecutor`, which is featured in the `concurrent.futures` module. In the previous example, in which we analyzed `parallel_fibonacci.py`, quite primitive forms of threads were used. Also, at a specific moment, we had to create and initialize more than one thread manually. In larger programs, it is very difficult to manage this kind of situation. In such case, there are mechanisms that allow a thread pool. A thread pool is nothing but a structure that keeps several threads, which are previously created, to be used in a certain process. It aims to reuse threads, thus avoiding unnecessary creation of threads — which is costly.

Basically, as mentioned in the previous chapter, we will have an algorithm that will execute some tasks in stages, and these tasks depend on each other. Here, we will study the code for our parallel Web crawler.

After importing some modules and setting up the logging file, we have created a regular expression using a built-in module called `re` (complete documentation on this module can be found at `http://docs.python.org/3/howto/regex.html`). We will use it to filter links in the pages that are returned from the crawling stage. The code is as follows:

```
html_link_regex = \
re.compile('<a\s(?:.*?\s)*?href=[\'"](.*?)[\'"].*?>')
```

Following the sequence, we have populated a synchronized queue so that it simulates certain input data. Then, we will declare a dictionary instance, which we will call `result_dict`. In this, we will correlate the URLs and their respective links as a list structure. The code is as follows:

```
urls = queue.Queue()
urls.put('http://www.google.com')
urls.put('http://br.bing.com/')
urls.put('https://duckduckgo.com/')
urls.put('https://github.com/')
urls.put('http://br.search.yahoo.com/')

result_dict = {}
```

In the following piece of code, a function called `group_urls_task` is defined to extract URLs from the synchronized queue to populate `result_dict`. We can see that the URLs are keys of `result_dict`. Another detail that we can observe is that the `get()` function was used with two arguments. The first argument is `True` to block the access to a synchronized queue. The second argument is a timeout of `0.05` to avoid this waiting getting too long in case of nonexistence of elements in the synchronized queue. In some cases, you do not want to spend too much time blocked in waiting for elements. The code is as follows:

```
def group_urls_task(urls):
    try:
        url = urls.get(True, 0.05)
        result_dict[url] = None
        logger.info("[%s] putting url [%s] in dictionary..." % (
            threading.current_thread().name, url))
    except queue.Empty:
        logging.error('Nothing to be done, queue is empty')
```

Now, we have the task that is responsible for accomplishing the crawling stage for each URL sent as an argument for the `crawl_task` function. Basically, the crawling stage is completed by obtaining all the links inside the page pointed by URL received. A tuple returned by crawling contains the first element as a URL received by the `crawl_task` function. As the second step, the list of links gets extracted. The `requests` module (the official documentation about the `request` module can be found at `https://pypi.python.org/pypi/requests`) was used to obtain the web pages from URLs. The code is as follows:

```
def crawl_task(url):
    links = []
    try:
        request_data = requests.get(url)
        logger.info("[%s] crawling url [%s] ..." % (
            threading.current_thread().name, url))
        links = html_link_regex.findall(request_data.text)
    except:
        logger.error(sys.exc_info()[0])
        raise
    finally:
        return (url, links)
```

Analyzing the code further, we will see the creation of an `ThreadPoolExecutor` object (more information about the `ThreadPoolExecutor` object can be found at `http://docs.python.org/3.3/library/concurrent.futures.html#concurrent.futures.ThreadPoolExecutor`) featured in the `concurrent.futures` module. In the constructor of this `ThreadPoolExecutor` object, we are able to define a parameter called `max_workers`. This parameter defines the number of threads in the thread pool attached to the executor. Within the stage of removal of the URLs from the synchronized queue and insertion of keys into `result_dict`, the choice was between using three worker threads. The quantity will vary according to the problem. After defining `ThreadPoolExecutor` and making use of the `with` statement to guarantee ending routines, these routines will be executed in the output of the scope of the `with` statement. In the `ThreadPoolExecutor` object's scope, we iterate it in the synchronized queue and dispatch it to execute a reference for the queue containing URLs by means of the `submit` method. Summing up, the `submit` method schedules a callable for the execution and returns a `Future` object containing the scheduling created for the execution. The `submit` method receives a callable and its arguments; in our case, the callable is the task `group_urls_task` and the argument is a reference to our synchronized queue. After these arguments are called, worker threads defined in the pool will execute the bookings in a parallel, asynchronous way. The code is as follows:

```
with concurrent.futures.ThreadPoolExecutor(max_workers=3) as\
    group_link_threads:
```

```
for i in range(urls.qsize()):
    group_link_threads.submit(group_urls_task, urls)
```

After the previous code, we created another `ThreadPoolExecutor`; but this time, we want to execute the crawling stage by using the keys generated by `group_urls_task` in the previous stage. This time, there is a difference in the following line:

```
future_tasks = {crawler_link_threads.submit(crawl_task, url): url
    for url in result_dict.keys()}
```

We have mapped a temporary dictionary called `future_tasks`. It will contain the bookings made by `submit`, passing by each URL featured in `result_dict`. That is, for each key, we create an entry in `future_tasks`. After mapping, we need to collect the results from the bookings as they are executed using a loop, which seeks completed entries in `future_tasks` using the `concurrent.futures.as_completed (fs, timeout=None)` method. This call returns an iterator for instances of the `Future` object. So, we can iterate in each result processed by the bookings that have been dispatched. At the end of `ThreadPoolExecutor`, for the crawling threads, we use the `result()` method from the `Future` object. In the case of the crawling stage, it returns the resulting tuple. In this way, we generate the final entries in `future_tasks` as shown in the following screenshot:

Crawling the Web in a parallel way

Once again, we can notice the order of the thread execution in each pool does not present a logical order, which is a consequence of non-determinism. The important thing is the printed items from `result_dict` showing the final result.

Summary

In this chapter, we have focused on a theoretical notion of the use of threads. We have implemented the examples that had been proposed in the previous chapter, making use of the `threading` module and `concurrent.futures`. In this way, we illustrated the module's mechanisms and flexibility.

In the next chapter, we will focus on how to solve these two problems using `multiprocessing` and `ProcessPoolExecutor`.

5
Using Multiprocessing and ProcessPoolExecutor

In the previous chapter, we studied how to use the threading module to solve two case problems. Throughout this present chapter, we will study how to use the multiprocessing module, which implements a similar interface to that of threading. However, here we will use the processes paradigm.

This chapter covers the following topics:

- Understanding the concept of a process
- Understanding multiprocessing communication
- Using multiprocessing to obtain Fibonacci series terms with multiple inputs
- Crawling the Web using ProcessPoolExecutor

Understanding the concept of a process

We must understand *processes* in operating systems as containers for programs in execution and their resources. All that is referring to a program in execution can be managed by means of the process it represents — its data area, its child processes, its estates, as well as its communication with other processes.

Understanding the process model

Processes have associated information and resources that allow their manipulation and control. The operating system has a structure called the **Process Control Block (PCB)**, which stores information referring to processes. For instance, the PCB might store the following information:

- **Process ID**: This is the unique integer value (unsigned) and which identifies a process within the operational system
- **Program counter**: This contains the address of the next program instruction to be executed
- **I/O information**: This is a list of open files and devices associated with the process
- **Memory allocation**: This stores information about the memory space used by and reserved for the process and the tables of paging
- **CPU scheduling**: This stores information about the priority of the process and points to the staggering queues
- **Priority**: This defines the priority that the process will have in the acquisition of the CPU
- **Current state**: This states whether the process is ready, waiting, or running
- **CPU registry**: This stores stack pointers and other information

Defining the states of a process

Processes possess three states that cross their life cycle; they are as follows:

- **Running**: The process is making use of the CPU
- **Ready**: The process that was waiting in the processes queue is now ready to use the CPU
- **Waiting**: The process is waiting for some I/O operation related to the task it was executing

Implementing multiprocessing communication

The `multiprocessing` module (`http://docs.python.org/3/library/multiprocessing.html`) allows two ways of communication among processes, both based on the message passing paradigm. As seen previously, the message passing paradigm is based on the lack of synchronizing mechanisms as copies of data are exchanged among processes.

Using multiprocessing.Pipe

A *pipe* consists of a mechanism that establishes communication between two *endpoints* (two processes in communication). It is a way to create a channel so as to exchange messages among processes.

 The official Python documentation recommends the use of a pipe for every two endpoints since there is no guarantee of reading safety by another endpoint simultaneously.

In order to exemplify the use of the `multiprocessing.Pipe` object, we will implement a Python program that creates two processes, A and B. Process A sends a random integer value in intervals from 1 to 10 to process B, and process B will display it on the screen. Now, let us check the program point by point.

Some essential modules have been imported to implement our example, as follows:

```
import os, random
from multiprocessing import Process, Pipe
```

The `os` module allows us to obtain the PID of the process, which executes a certain point of the program by using `os.getpid()` (http://docs.python.org/3.3/library/os.html). The `os.getpid()` call will return in a transparent form in our example. It will return the PID of the respective processes responsible for running tasks `producer_task` and `consumer_task`.

In the next part of the program, we will define the `producer_task` function, which, among other things, will generate a random number using the `random.randint(1, 10)` call. The key point of this function is called `conn.send(value)`, which uses a connection object generated by `Pipe` in the flux of the main program that has been sent as an argument to the function. Observe the full body of the `producer_task` function as follows:

```
def producer_task(conn):
    value = random.randint(1, 10)
    conn.send(value)
    print('Value [%d] sent by PID [%d]' % (value, os.getpid()))
    conn.close()
```

 Never forget to always call the `close()` method of a `Pipe` connection which sends data through the `send` method. This is important to finalize resources associated with the channel of communication when this is no longer being used.

The task to be executed by the consumer process is quite simple, and its only goal is to print the received value on screen, informing the PID of the consuming process. To obtain the sent value from a channel of communication, we used the `conn.recv()` call (http://docs.python.org/dev/library/multiprocessing.html#multiprocessing.Connection.recv). The implementation of the `consumer_task` function ended up like the following:

```
def consumer_task(conn):
    print('Value [%d] received by PID [%d]' % (conn.recv(),
    os.getpid()))
```

The final part of our little example realizes a call to the `Pipe()` object by creating two connection objects that will be used by the consumer and producer processes. After this call, the producer and consumer processes are created, sending the `consumer_task` and `producer_task` functions as target functions respectively, as we may observe in the following full code:

```
if __name__ == '__main__':
    producer_conn, consumer_conn = Pipe()
    consumer = Process(target=consumer_task,args=(consumer_conn,))
    producer = Process(target=producer_task,args=(producer_conn,))

    consumer.start()
    producer.start()

    consumer.join()
    producer.join()
```

After defining the processes, it is time to make a call to the `start()` method to initiate the execution and the `join()` method so that the main process waits for the execution of the producer and consumer processes.

In the following screenshot, we can see the output of the `multiprocessing_pipe.py` program:

Output from multiprocessing_pipe.py

Understanding multiprocessing.Queue

In the previous section, we analyzed the concept of a pipe to establish communication among processes by creating a communication channel. Now, we will be analyzing how to effectively establish this communication, making use of the Queue object, which is implemented in the multiprocessing module. The available interfaces for multiprocessing.Queue are quite similar to queue.Queue. However, the internal implementation uses different mechanisms, such as an internal thread called **feeder thread**, which transfers data from the data buffer of the queue to the pipes associated with the destination processes. Both the Pipe and Queue mechanisms make use of the message passing paradigm, which spares users from the need to use synchronization mechanisms.

> Although the user of multiprocessing.Queue does not need to use synchronization mechanisms, such as Locks for instance, but internally, these mechanisms are used to transport data among buffers and pipes in order to accomplish communication.

Using multiprocessing to compute Fibonacci series terms with multiple inputs

Let's implement the case study of processing a Fibonacci series for multiple inputs using the processes approach instead of threads.

The multiprocessing_fibonacci.py code makes use of the multiprocessing module, and in order to run, it imports some essential modules as we can observe in the following code:

```
import sys, time, random, re, requests
import concurrent.futures
from multiprocessing import, cpu_count, current_process, Manager
```

Some imports have been mentioned in the previous chapters; nevertheless, some of the following imports do deserve special attention:

- cpu_count: This is a function that permits obtaining the quantity of CPUs in a machine

- current_process: This is a function that allows obtaining information on the current process, for example, its name

- `Manager`: This is a type of object that allows sharing Python objects among different processes by means of proxies (for more information, see http://docs.python.org/3/library/multiprocessing.html)

Following the code, we can notice that the first function will behave differently; it will generate random values in an interval from 1 to 20 during 0-14 iterations. These values will be inserted as keys in `fibo_dict`, a dictionary generated by a `Manager` object.

> It is more common to use the message passing approach. However, in some cases, we need to share a piece of data among different processes as we can see on our `fibo_dict` dictionary.

Let's now check the `producer_task` method, as follows:

```
def producer_task(q, fibo_dict):
    for i in range(15):
        value = random.randint(1, 20)
        fibo_dict[value] = None

        logger.info("Producer [%s] putting value [%d] into
            queue.. " % (current_process().name, value))
        q.put(value)
```

The next step is to define the function that will calculate the Fibonacci series term for each key in `fibo_dict`. It is noticeable that the only difference in relation to the function presented in the previous chapter is the use of `fibo_dict` as an argument to enable its use by different processes.

Let us check the `consumer_task` function, as follows:

```
def consumer_task(q, fibo_dict):
    while not q.empty():
        value = q.get(True, 0.05)
        a, b = 0, 1
        for item in range(value):
            a, b = b, a + b
            fibo_dict[value] = a
        logger.info("consumer [%s] getting value [%d] from
            queue..." % (current_process().name, value))
```

Going further with the code, we enter the main block of the program. In this main block, some of the following variables are defined:

- `data_queue`: This contains `multiprocessing.Queue` that is processed safely by the standard

- `number_of_cpus`: This contains the value returned by the `multiprocessing.cpu_count` function as explained earlier

- `fibo_dict`: This is a dictionary generated by the `Manager` object, where the final results of the process will be inserted

Further in the code, we have created a process called `producer` to populate `data_queue` with random values using the `producer_task` function, as follows:

```
producer = Process(target=producer_task, args=(data_queue,
    fibo_dict))
producer.start()
producer.join()
```

We can observe that the signature on the initializer of the `Process` class is the same as the one used on the `Thread` class, which is present in the `threading` package. It receives a target function to be executed in parallel by the workers and the arguments for this function. Then, we started the process execution and made a call to the `join()` method so that the main process goes on only after the conclusion of the `producer` process.

In the next chunk, we defined a list called `consumer_list`, which will store a list of consumers with their processes already initialized. The reason for creating this list is to call `join()` only after the beginning of the processes of all the workers. If the `join()` function was called for each item in the loop, then only the first worker would perform the job as the next iteration would be blocked waiting for the current worker to end, and finally there would be nothing else to be processed by the next worker; the following code represents this scenario:

```
consumer_list = []
for i in range(number_of_cpus):
    consumer = Process(target=consumer_task, args=(data_queue,
        fibo_dict))
    consumer.start()
    consumer_list.append(consumer)

[consumer.join() for consumer in consumer_list]
```

Eventually, we presented the result iterating in `fibo_dict`, as shown in the following screenshot:

```
2014-05-13 16:01:13,424 - Producer [Process-2] putting value [13] into queue..
2014-05-13 16:01:13,436 - consumer [Process-3] getting value [1] from queue...
2014-05-13 16:01:13,439 - consumer [Process-3] getting value [17] from queue...
2014-05-13 16:01:13,441 - consumer [Process-3] getting value [16] from queue...
2014-05-13 16:01:13,443 - consumer [Process-3] getting value [20] from queue...
2014-05-13 16:01:13,449 - consumer [Process-3] getting value [14] from queue...
2014-05-13 16:01:13,459 - consumer [Process-4] getting value [10] from queue...
2014-05-13 16:01:13,465 - consumer [Process-5] getting value [6] from queue...
2014-05-13 16:01:13,468 - consumer [Process-6] getting value [7] from queue...
2014-05-13 16:01:13,469 - consumer [Process-5] getting value [14] from queue...
2014-05-13 16:01:13,470 - consumer [Process-5] getting value [2] from queue...
2014-05-13 16:01:13,472 - consumer [Process-4] getting value [19] from queue...
2014-05-13 16:01:13,472 - consumer [Process-6] getting value [17] from queue...
2014-05-13 16:01:13,474 - consumer [Process-3] getting value [12] from queue...
2014-05-13 16:01:13,477 - consumer [Process-4] getting value [13] from queue...
2014-05-13 16:01:13,478 - consumer [Process-5] getting value [19] from queue...
2014-05-13 16:01:13,481 - {1: 1, 2: 1, 6: 8, 7: 13, 10: 55, 12: 144, 13: 233, 14: 377, 16: 987,
yipman@foshan:~/Documents/prog_experiments/python/8397_05_1stDraft$
```

Output from multiprocessing_fibonacci.py

Crawling the Web using ProcessPoolExecutor

Just as the `concurrent.futures` module offers `ThreadPoolExecutor`, which facilitates the creation and manipulation of multiple threads, processes belong to the class of `ProcessPoolExecutor`. The `ProcessPoolExecutor` class, which also featured in the `concurrent.futures` pack, was used to implement our parallel Web crawler. In order to implement this case study, we have created a Python module named `process_pool_executor_web_crawler.py`.

The code initiates with the imports known from the previous examples, such as `requests`, the `Manager` module, and so on. In relation to the definition of the tasks, and referring to the use of threads, little has changed compared to the example from the previous chapter, except that now we send data to be manipulated by means of function arguments; refer to the following signatures:

The `group_urls_task` function is defined as follows:

```
def group_urls_task(urls, result_dict, html_link_regex)
```

The `crawl_task` function is defined as follows:

```
def crawl_task(url, html_link_regex)
```

Let's now look at a chunk of the code where there are subtle but relevant changes. Entering the main chunk, we declared an object of the type `Manager`, which will now allow the sharing of the queue and not only the dictionary containing the process result. To define this queue named `urls` containing the URLs that need to be crawled, we will use the `Manager.Queue` object. For the `result_dictionary`, we will use the `Manager.dict` object aiming to use a dictionary managed by proxies. The following chunk of code illustrates these definitions:

```python
if __name__ == '__main__':
    manager = Manager()
    urls = manager.Queue()
    urls.put('http://www.google.com')
    urls.put('http://br.bing.com/')
    urls.put('https://duckduckgo.com/')
    urls.put('https://github.com/')
    urls.put('http://br.search.yahoo.com/')
    result_dict = manager.dict()
```

Then, we defined the regular expression to be used in the crawler stage, and we obtained the number of processors in the machine that run the program as shown in the following code

```python
html_link_regex = \
    re.compile('<a\s(?:.*?\s)*?href=[\'"](.*?)[\'"].*?>')

number_of_cpus = cpu_count()
```

In the final chunk, we can notice the consistency in the APIs that are in the `concurrent.futures` module. The following chunk is exactly the one used in our example using `ThreadPoolExecutor`, as mentioned in the previous chapter. However, it is enough to change the class to `ProcessPoolExecutor` by altering the internal behavior and tackling the GIL issue for CPU-bound processes without breaking the code. Check the following chunks; both create `ProcessPoolExecutor` with workers with limits equal to the number of processors in the machine. The first executor is for grouping the URLs in the dictionary with the standard `None` value.
The second executor proceeds with the crawling stage.

The following is the chunk of code for executor 1:

```python
with concurrent.futures.ProcessPoolExecutor(
    max_workers=number_of_cpus) as group_link_processes:
        for i in range(urls.qsize()):
            group_link_processes.submit(group_urls_task, urls,
                result_dict, html_link_regex)
```

The following is the chunk of code for executor 2:

```
with concurrent.futures.ProcessPoolExecutor(
    max_workers=number_of_cpus) as crawler_link_processes:
        future_tasks = {crawler_link_processes.submit(crawl_task,
            url, html_link_regex):
            url for url in result_dict.keys()}
        for future in concurrent.futures.as_completed(
            future_tasks):
            result_dict[future.result()[0]] = future.result()[1]
```

 Keying from the multithreaded paradigm to `multiprocess` using `concurrent.futures` is somewhat simpler.

We can check the program output `process_pool_executor_web_crawler.py` as shown in the following screenshot:

```
yipman@foshan:~/Documents/prog_experiments/python/8397_05_1stDraft$ /opt/python
[Process-2] putting url [http://www.google.com] in dictionary...
[Process-3] putting url [http://br.bing.com/] in dictionary...
[Process-4] putting url [https://duckduckgo.com/] in dictionary...
[Process-5] putting url [https://github.com/] in dictionary...
[Process-2] putting url [http://br.search.yahoo.com/] in dictionary...
[Process-9] crawling url [http://www.google.com] ...
[Process-6] crawling url [http://br.search.yahoo.com/] ...
[Process-8] crawling url [http://br.bing.com/] ...
[Process-7] crawling url [https://duckduckgo.com/] ...
[Process-9] crawling url [https://github.com/] ...
[https://duckduckgo.com/] with links : [/about...
[http://br.search.yahoo.com/] with links : [https://br.yahoo.com/...
[http://www.google.com] with links : [http://www.google.com.br/imghp?hl=pt-BR&t
[http://br.bing.com/] with links : [/account/web?sh=5&amp;ru=%2f...
[https://github.com/] with links : [#start-of-content...
yipman@foshan:~/Documents/prog_experiments/python/8397_05_1stDraft$
```

Output from process_pool_executor_web_crawler.py

Summary

In this chapter, we observed the general concepts about processes and implemented case studies using the multiple processes approach to compute the Fibonacci series terms and the Web crawler in a parallel way.

In the next chapter, we will look at multiple processes using the *parallel Python* module, which is not a built-in module within Python. We will learn about the concept of inter-process communication and how to use pipes to communicate between processes.

6
Utilizing Parallel Python

In the previous chapter, we learned how to use the `multiprocessing` and `ProcessPoolExecutor` modules to solve two case problems. This chapter will present named pipes and how to use **Parallel Python** (**PP**) to perform parallel tasks with processes.

In this chapter, we will cover the following topics:

- Understanding interprocess communication
- Discovering PP
- Using PP to calculate the Fibonacci series on SMP architecture
- Using PP to make a distributed Web crawler

Understanding interprocess communication

Interprocess communication (**IPC**) consists of mechanisms that allow the exchange of information among processes.

There are several means to implement IPC, and in general, they depend on the chosen architecture for the runtime environment. In some cases, for example, where processes run on the same machine, we could use various types of communication, such as shared memory, message queues, and pipes. When processes are physically distributed in clusters, for instance, we could use sockets and **Remote Procedure Call** (**RPC**).

In *Chapter 5, Using Multiprocessing and ProcessPoolExecutor*, we verified the use of regular pipes among other things. We also studied the communication among processes that have a common parent process. But, sometimes it is necessary to perform communication between unrelated processes (processes with different parent processes). We might ask ourselves if the communication between unrelated processes could be done through their addressing space. Nevertheless, a process never accesses the addressing space from another process. Thus, we must use mechanisms called named pipes.

Exploring named pipes

Within the POSIX systems, such as Linux, we should keep in mind that everything, absolutely everything, can be summed up to files. For each task we perform, there is a file somewhere, and we can also find a `file` descriptor attached to it, which allows us to manipulate these files.

 File descriptors are mechanisms that allow the user programs to access files for read/write operations. Normally, a file is referenced by a unique file descriptor. More information about the file descriptors can be found at `http://publib.boulder.ibm.com/infocenter/pseries/v5r3/index.jsp?topic=/com.ibm.aix.genprogc/doc/genprogc/fdescript.htm`.

Named pipes are nothing but mechanisms that allow IPC communication through the use of file descriptors associated with special files that implement, for instance, a **First-In, First-Out (FIFO)** scheme for writing and reading the data. Named pipes differ from regular pipes by the method with which they manage information. While the named pipes make use of the file descriptors and special files in a file system, regular pipes are created in memory.

Using named pipes with Python

The use of named pipes in Python is quite simple, and we will illustrate this by implementing two programs performing unidirectional communication. The first program is named `write_to_named_pipe.py`, and its function is to write a message in the pipe with 22 bytes, informing a string and PID of the process that generated it. The second program is called `read_from_named_pipe.py`, and it will perform the reading of the information and will show the message content, adding its PID.

At the end of the execution, the `read_from_named_pipe.py` process will show **I pid [<The PID of reader process>] received a message => Hello from pid [the PID of writer process]**.

To illustrate the interdependency between writing and reading the processes in a named pipe, we will execute the reader and writer in two distinct consoles. But before checking the result, let's analyze the codes for both programs.

Writing in a named pipe

In Python, named pipes are implemented through the `system` calls. In the following code, we will explain the functioning of the `write_to_named_pipe.py` program line by line.

We start with the input of the `os` module, which will provide access to the system calls we will use the following line of code:

```
import os
```

According to the code, we will explain the __main__ chunk that creates the named pipe and a special file, FIFO, which stores messages. The first line of the __main__ chunk defines the label we will give to our named pipe, as follows:

```
named_pipe = "my_pipe"
```

Then, we verify that our named pipe already exists. In the case that it does not, we will create it by means of the system call, `mkfifo`, as follows:

```
if not os.path.exists(named_pipe):
    os.mkfifo(named_pipe)
```

The `mkfifo` call creates a special file that implements a FIFO mechanism for the writing and reading of messages through a named pipe.

Now, we call our `write_message` function to pass the `named_pipe` argument and a `Hello from pid [%d]` message. This function will write the message in a file managed by the named pipe received as an argument. The definition of the `write_message` function can be seen as follows:

```
def write_message(input_pipe, message):
    fd = os.open(input_pipe, os.O_WRONLY)
    os.write(fd, (message % str(os.getpid())))
    os.close(fd)
```

We can observe that in the first line of the function, we have a call to a system call, `open`, which, in the event of its success, returns a file descriptor that allows us to manage the writing and reading of data in the FIFO file. Notice that we can control the opening mode of our FIFO file by using flags. As for the `write_message` function, it is interesting to only write data in it. Refer to the following code:

```
fd = os.open(input_pipe, os.O_WRONLY)
```

After the successful opening of the named pipe, we write the message in the channel informed by the PID of the writer process as follows:

```
os.write(fd, (message % os.getpid()))
```

At the end, it is important to close the communication channel using the `close` call as follows. In this way, the communication and freeing the computer resources are involved:

```
os.close(fd)
```

Reading named pipes

To read our named pipe, we have implemented a Python program called `read_from_pipe.py`, which uses the `os` module to manipulate the named pipes. The `main` chunk, which triggers the process, is simple. We define a label to the named pipe we will use. In this case, the same named pipe is used in the writing program as follows:

```
named_pipe = "my_pipe"
```

Then, we call the `read_message` function, which will read the content written by `write_to_named_pipe.py`. The definition of the `read_message` function can be seen as follows:

```
def read_message(input_type):
    fd = os.open(input_pipe, os_RONLY)
    message = (
        "I pid [%d] received a message => %s"
            % (os.getpid(), os.read(fd, 22))
    os.close(fd)
    return message
```

The `open` call needs no introduction. The new thing here is our `read` call, which performs the reading of a quantity in bytes. In our case, it is 22 bytes if a file descriptor is given. After the message is read, it is returned by the function. At the end, the `close` call must be executed to close the communication channel.

 The validity of the open file descriptor was verified. It is up to the user to deal with the exceptions related to the use of file descriptors and named pipes.

As a result, we have the following screenshot illustrating the execution of the `write_to_named_pipe` and `read_from_named_pipe` programs:

Result from write_to_named_pipe.py and read_from_named_pipe.py

Discovering PP

The previous section introduced a low-level mechanism to establish communication among the processes using system calls directly. This was necessary to contextualize the communication between processes in the Linux and Unix environments. Now, we will use a Python module, PP, to establish IPC communication not only among local processes, but also physically distributed throughout a computer network.

The available PP module documentation is not extensive. We can find the documents and FAQs at `http://www.parallelpython.com/component/option,com_smf/`. The API provides a wide notion of how this tool should be used; it is simple and straightforward.

The most important advantage of using PP is the abstraction that this module provides. Some important features of PP are as follows:

- Automatic detection of number of processors to improve load balance
- Many processors allocated can be changed at runtime
- Load balance at runtime
- Auto-discovery resources throughout the network

The PP module implements the execution of parallel code in two ways. The first way considers the SMP architecture, where there are multiple processors/cores in the same machine. The second alternative would be distributing the tasks through machines in a network, configuring, and thus forming a cluster. In both cases, the exchange of information among the processes receives a call of abstraction, which allows us not to worry about details such as pipes and sockets. We simply exchange the information through arguments and function returns using callbacks. Refer to the following example.

There is a class, called `Server`, present in the API of PP, which we can use to encapsulate and dispatch tasks among local and remote processes. There are some important arguments in the initializer (__init__) from the `Server` class. The most relevant arguments are as follows:

- `ncpus`: This argument allows us to define the number of worker processes, which will execute tasks. If a value is not informed, it will automatically detect how many processors/cores the machine has and create a total of worker processes based on this to optimize the use of resources.

- `ppservers`: This argument represents a tuple containing names or IP addresses of machines that we call **Parallel Python Execution Servers** (**PPES**). A PPES consists of a network machine that has the `ppserver.py` utility running and waiting for tasks to be executed. There are other arguments that can be visualized at `http://www.parallelpython.com/content/view/15/30/`.

  An instance of the `Server` class has, among several methods, the `submit` method that allows us to dispatch tasks to their destinations. The `submit` function has the following signature:

```
submit(self, func, args=(), depfuncs=(), modules=(),
    callback=None, callbackargs=(), group='default',
        globals=None)
```

Among the `main` arguments of the `submit` method, we could highlight the following parameters:

- `func`: This function is executed by the local processes or remote servers.

- `args`: This function executes the necessary arguments for the `func` function.

- `modules`: This function executes the modules that the remote code or process needs to import for the execution of `func`. For example, if the dispatched function uses the `time` module, in the `tuple` modules, a string with this module name has to be passed as `modules=('time', )`.

- `callback`: This is a function we will make use of later on. It is very interesting when we need to manipulate results of the process from the function dispatched in the `func` argument. The return of the dispatched function is sent as an argument to callback.

Other arguments will be featured as we analyze the code for the next sections.

Using PP to calculate the Fibonacci series term on SMP architecture

Time to get into action! Let's solve our case study involving the Fibonacci series for multiple inputs using PP in the SMP architecture. I am using a notebook armed with a two-core processor and four threads.

We will import only two modules for this implementation, os and pp. The os module will be used only to obtain a PID of the processes in execution. We will have a list called input_list with the values to be calculated and a dictionary to group the results, which we will call result_dict. Then, we go to the chunk of code as follows:

```
import os, pp
input_list = [4, 3, 8, 6, 10]
result_dict = {}
```

Then, we define a function called fibo_task, which will be executed by parallel processes. It will be our func argument passed by the submit method of the Server class. The function does not feature major changes in relation to previous chapters, except that the return is now done by using a tuple to encapsulate the value received in the argument and a message containing a PID and a calculated Fibonacci term. Take a look at the following complete function:

```
def fibo_task(value):
    a, b = 0, 1
    for item in range(value):
        a, b = b, a + b
    message = "the fibonacci calculated by pid %d was %d" \
        % (os.getpid(), a)
    return (value, message)
```

The next step is to define our callback function, which we will call aggregate_results. The callback function will be called as soon as the fibo_task function returns the result of its execution. Its implementation is quite simple and only shows a status message, generating afterwards an input in result_dict, containing as a key the value passed to the fibo_dict function, and as a result, the message returned by the process that calculated the Fibonacci term. The following code is the complete implementation of the aggregate_results function:

```
def aggregate_results(result):
    print "Computing results with PID [%d]" % os.getpid()
    result_dict[result[0]] = result[1]
```

Now, we have two functions to be defined. We have to create an instance of the Server class to dispatch the tasks. The following line of code creates an instance of Server:

```
job_server = pp.Server()
```

In the preceding example, we used standard values for arguments. In the next section, we will make use of some available arguments.

Now that we have an instance of the Server class, let's iterate each value of our input_list, dispatching the fibo_task function through the submit call, passing as arguments to the input value in the args tuple the module that needs to be imported so that the function is executed correctly and callback registers aggregate_results. Refer to the following chunk of code:

```
for item in input_list:
    job_server.submit(fibo_task, (item,), modules=('os',),
        callback=aggregate_results)
```

Finally, we have to wait till the end of all the dispatched tasks. Therefore, we can use the wait method of the Server class as follows:

```
job_server.wait()
```

 There is another way to obtain the return of an executed function beyond using a callback function. The submit method returns an object type, pp._Task, which contains the result of the execution when the execution finishes.

In the end, we will iterate the results of the printing entries through our dictionary as follows:

```
print "Main process PID [%d]" % os.getpid()
for key, value in result_dict.items():
    print "For input %d, %s" % (key, value)
```

The following screenshot illustrates the output of the program:

```
iceman@iceman-ThinkPad-X220: ~/Documentos/8307_06_pp_codes
iceman@iceman-ThinkPad-X220:~/Documentos/8307_06_pp_codes$ python fibonacci_pp_smp.py
Computing results with PID [23467]
Computing results with PID [23467]
Computing results with PID [23467]
Computing results with PID [23467]
Computing results with PID [23467]
Main process PID [23467]
For input 8, the fibonacci calculated by pid 23470 was 21
For input 10, the fibonacci calculated by pid 23468 was 55
For input 3, the fibonacci calculated by pid 23469 was 2
For input 4, the fibonacci calculated by pid 23468 was 3
For input 6, the fibonacci calculated by pid 23471 was 8
iceman@iceman-ThinkPad-X220:~/Documentos/8307_06_pp_codes$
```

Result from fibonacci_pp_smp.py

Using PP to make a distributed Web crawler

Now that we have executed the codes in parallel using PP to dispatch the local processes, it is time to verify that the code is executed in a distributed way. For this, we will use the following three different machines:

- **Iceman-Thinkad-X220**: Ubuntu 13.10
- **Iceman-Q47OC-500P4C**: Ubuntu 12.04 LTS
- **Asgard-desktop**: Elementary OS

The idea is to dispatch the executions to the three machines listed using PP. For this, we will make use of a case study of the Web crawler. In the code of web_crawler_pp_cluster.py, for each URL informed in the input_list, we will dispatch a local or remote process for execution, and at the end of each execution, a callback function will group the URLs and their first three links found.

Let us analyze the code step by step to understand how to get to a solution to this problem. First, we will import the necessary modules and define the data structures to be used. As in the previous section, we will create an input_list and a dictionary that will contain the final results of processing. Refer to the following code:

```
import os, re, requests, pp

url_list = ['http://www.google.com/','http://gizmodo.uol.com.br/',
    'https://github.com/', 'http://br.search.yahoo.com/',
    'http://www.python.org/','http://www.python.org/psf/']

result_dict = {}
```

Now, our `aggregate_results` function, which will be our callback again, changes little in relation to the example presented for the Fibonacci term. We only changed the format of the message to be inserted in the dictionary and also the fact that the return to this callback will be a tuple containing the PID of the process that executed it, the hostname where it was executed, and the first three links found. Refer to the `aggregate_results` function as follows:

```
def aggregate_results(result):
    print "Computing results in main process PID [%d]" %
        os.getpid()
    message = "PID %d in hostname [%s] the following links were "\
        "found: %s" % (result[2], result[3], result[1])
    result_dict[result[0]] = message
```

The next step is to define the `crawl_task` function, which will be dispatched by an instance of the `Server` class. The function is similar to the one presented in previous chapters, aiming to gather existing links in the page shown by the URL received as an argument. The only difference is that the return is a tuple. Refer to the following code:

```
def crawl_task(url):
    html_link_regex = \
    re.compile('<a\s(?:.*?\s)*?href=[\'"](.*?)[\'"].*?>')

    request_data = requests.get(url)
    links = html_link_regex.findall(request_data.text)[:3]
    return (url, links, os.getpid(), os.uname()[1])
```

After the `main` and `callback` functions are written, we must create an instance of the `Server` class to distribute the executions in the machines through the network. For this, we will work on some arguments in the initializer of the `Server` class. The first argument receives a tuple with the IP addresses or hostnames of the machines that will execute tasks. In our case, beyond the local machine, we will inform the two others presented previously. Let us define the tuple as follows:

```
ppservers = ("192.168.25.21", "192.168.25.9")
```

> In case you do not want to inform and wish to autodiscover the machines available to receive tasks, use the * string in the ppservers tuple.

Define the tuple identifying the servers. We will create an instance of `Server` as follows:

```
job_dispatcher = pp.Server(ncpus=1, ppservers=ppservers,
    socket_timeout=60000)
```

It is noticeable that there are some changes in relation to the previous example. First, we have passed the value 1 to the ncpus argument. This will cause PP to create a single local process, and if necessary, dispatch other tasks to remote machines. The second argument defined was the tuple of the servers we created in the previous step. Finally, we defined a timeout for the socket(s) used in the communication with a pretty high value only for the purposes of testing. The goal is to avoid the closing of the channel by timeout.

After an instance of the Server class is created, it is time to dispatch our functions for execution. Let us iterate in each URL and pass them to the submit method of the Server instance as follows:

```
for url in url_list:
    job_dispatcher.submit(crawl_task, (url,),
        modules=('os', 're', 'requests',),
            callback=aggregate_results)
```

The significant change in relation to the previous example, where a Fibonacci series was calculated, is the sending of the necessary modules for execution.

You must be thinking why the PP module has not been passed in the tuple module. It is simple; the PP execution environment already makes this import for us. After all, it needs to do this in remote nodes.

To finalize our parallel and distributed Web crawlers, we have to wait till the end of the executions to show their outputs. Notice that by the end, there is a new element in the print_stats method of the Server class, which shows some interesting statistics of the executions as follows:

```
job_dispatcher.wait()

print "\nMain process PID [%d]\n" % os.getpid()
for key, value in result_dict.items():
    print "** For url %s, %s\n" % (key, value)
    job_dispatcher.print_stats()
```

Before executing the program, we need to initialize the ppserver.py utility in the remote machines; ppserver.py -a -d is the command used here for this, where -a is the option for autodiscovery, allowing the server to be found by clients who do not specify the IP address. The other argument is -d, which shows the information on how the activities of the server are performing by means of a log.

Let us visualize the output in the following order:

- First, the following screenshot shows the stages in the `main` node, which creates and distributes tasks:

```
iceman@iceman-ThinkPad-X220:~/Documentos/8307_06_pp_codes$ python2.7 web_crawler_pp_cluster.py
Computing results in main process PID [17027]
Computing results in main process PID [17027]
Computing results in main process PID [17027]
Computing results in main process PID [17027]
** For url http://gizmodo.uol.com.br/, PID 23639 in hostname [iceman-Q470C-500P4C] the following links were
found: [u'http://trivela.uol.com.br/', u'http://www.kotaku.com.br/', u'http://extratime.uol.com.br/']

** For url http://br.search.yahoo.com/, PID 23640 in hostname [iceman-Q470C-500P4C] the following links were
found: [u'http://br.yahoo.com/', u'http://br.images.search.yahoo.com/search/images?&fr=brsfp2', u'http://br
.video.search.yahoo.com/video?&fr=sfp']

** For url http://www.google.com/, PID 17030 in hostname [iceman-ThinkPad-X220] the following links were fou
nd: [u'http://www.google.com.br/imghp?hl=pt-BR&tab=wi', u'http://maps.google.com.br/maps?hl=pt-BR&tab=wl', u
'https://play.google.com/?hl=pt-BR&tab=w8']

** For url https://github.com/, PID 19543 in hostname [asgard-desktop] the following links were found: [u'ht
tps://github.com/', u'/join', u'/login']

Job execution statistics:
 job count | % of all jobs | job time sum | time per job | job server
    2 |         50.00 |       1.8652 |     0.932602 | 192.168.25.21:60000
    1 |         25.00 |       0.6687 |     0.668653 | local
    1 |         25.00 |       1.6741 |     1.674122 | 192.168.25.9:60000
Time elapsed since server creation 2.13039803505
0 active tasks, 1 cores

None
iceman@iceman-ThinkPad-X220:~/Documentos/8307_06_pp_codes$
```

Creating and distributing tasks

- Then, the `ppservers.py` server is initialized and the processing tasks are seen in the following screenshots (*Output from ppserver.py at iceman-Q47OC-500P4C* and *Output from ppserver.py at asgard-desktop*).

- In the preceding screenshot, it is noticeable that the statistics bring about interesting information, such as the quantity of tasks that have been distributed among different destinations, the timing of each task, and the total in each destination. Another relevant point in the preceding screenshot is the fact that the `callback` functions are only executed in the main process, the ones in the dispatching tasks. So, it is important to keep in mind that you should not make the callback tasks excessively heavy, as they may consume too many resources from the `main` node; it obviously depends on the specifics of each case.

- The following screenshot shows the output in the `DEBUG` mode of the `ppserver.py` server executing in host `iceman-Q47OC-500P4C`:

```
iceman@iceman-Q470C-500P4C:~$ ppserver.py -a -d
2014-02-11 10:49:54,487 - pp - INFO - Creating server instance (pp-1.6.4)
2014-02-11 10:49:54,487 - pp - INFO - Running on Python 2.7.3 linux2
2014-02-11 10:49:54,713 - pp - INFO - pp local server started with 4 workers
2014-02-11 10:49:54,713 - pp - DEBUG - Strarting network server interface=0.0.0.0 port=60000
2014-02-11 10:49:54,714 - pp - DEBUG - Listening (0.0.0.0, 60000)
2014-02-11 10:49:54,715 - pp - DEBUG - Server sends broadcast to (255.255.255.255, 60000)
2014-02-11 10:49:54,715 - pp - DEBUG - Discovered host (192.168.25.21, 60000) message=S
2014-02-11 10:49:56,426 - pp - DEBUG - Discovered host (192.168.25.9, 60000) message=S
2014-02-11 10:50:00,430 - pp - DEBUG - Control message received: STAT
2014-02-11 10:50:00,575 - pp - DEBUG - Control message received: EXEC
2014-02-11 10:50:00,625 - pp - DEBUG - Control message received: EXEC
2014-02-11 10:50:00,691 - pp - DEBUG - Control message received: EXEC
2014-02-11 10:50:00,775 - pp - DEBUG - Control message received: EXEC
2014-02-11 10:50:00,777 - pp - DEBUG - Task 0 inserted
2014-02-11 10:50:00,777 - pp - DEBUG - Task 1 inserted
2014-02-11 10:50:00,778 - pp - INFO - Task 0 started
2014-02-11 10:50:00,779 - pp - INFO - Task 1 started
2014-02-11 10:50:00,808 - pp - DEBUG - Control message received: EXEC
2014-02-11 10:50:00,878 - pp - DEBUG - Control message received: EXEC
2014-02-11 10:50:00,942 - pp - DEBUG - Control message received: EXEC
2014-02-11 10:50:01,013 - pp - DEBUG - Control message received: EXEC
2014-02-11 10:50:01,514 - pp - DEBUG - Task 0 ended
2014-02-11 10:50:01,911 - pp - DEBUG - Task 1 ended
2014-02-11 10:50:04,723 - pp - DEBUG - Server sends broadcast to (255.255.255.255, 60000)
2014-02-11 10:50:04,723 - pp - DEBUG - Discovered host (192.168.25.21, 60000) message=S
2014-02-11 10:50:06,506 - pp - DEBUG - Discovered host (192.168.25.9, 60000) message=S
^C2014-02-11 10:50:12,731 - pp - DEBUG - Closing server socket
iceman@iceman-Q470C-500P4C:~$ 
```

Output from ppserver.py at iceman-Q47OC-500P4C

- The following screenshot shows the output in the DEBUG mode of the ppserver.py server executing in the asgard-desktop host:

```
2014-02-11 10:50:02,701 - pp - DEBUG - Closing client socket
DEBUG:pp:Closing client socket
2014-02-11 10:50:02,702 - pp - DEBUG - Closing client socket
DEBUG:pp:Closing client socket
2014-02-11 10:50:02,702 - pp - DEBUG - Closing client socket
DEBUG:pp:Closing client socket
2014-02-11 10:50:02,702 - pp - DEBUG - Closing client socket
DEBUG:pp:Closing client socket
2014-02-11 10:50:06,527 - pp - DEBUG - Server sends broadcast to (255.255.255.255, 60000)
DEBUG:pp:Server sends broadcast to (255.255.255.255, 60000)
2014-02-11 10:50:06,527 - pp - DEBUG - Discovered host (192.168.25.9, 60000) message=S
DEBUG:pp:Discovered host (192.168.25.9, 60000) message=S
2014-02-11 10:50:16,537 - pp - DEBUG - Server sends broadcast to (255.255.255.255, 60000)
DEBUG:pp:Server sends broadcast to (255.255.255.255, 60000)
2014-02-11 10:50:16,538 - pp - DEBUG - Discovered host (192.168.25.9, 60000) message=S
DEBUG:pp:Discovered host (192.168.25.9, 60000) message=S
^C2014-02-11 10:50:19,609 - pp - DEBUG - Closing server socket
DEBUG:pp:Closing server socket
iceman@asgard-desktop:~$ 
```

Output from ppserver.py at asgard-desktop

Summary

We studied the use of a low-level resource to establish communication among processes with no relation between them. Further, we have taken a look at using the PP module, which helps us abstract the communication among the local processes, including distributed processes. PP is a convenient tool for building simple, small, parallel, and distributed Python applications.

In the next chapter, we will learn how to use a module called **Celery** for the execution of tasks in a parallel and distributed way.

Distributing Tasks with Celery

In the previous chapter, we learned about using parallel Python. We saw the implementation of case studies, including Fibonacci series terms and Web crawler using the parallel Python module. We learned how to establish communication among processes using pipes and how to distribute processes among different machines in a network. In this chapter, we will study how to distribute tasks among different machines in a network by using the *Celery* framework.

In this chapter, we will cover the following topics:

- Understanding Celery
- Understanding Celery's architecture
- Setting up the environment
- Dispatching a simple task
- Using Celery to obtain a Fibonacci series term
- Using Celery to make a distributed Web crawler

Understanding Celery

Celery is a framework that offers mechanisms to lessen difficulties while creating distributed systems. The Celery framework works with the concept of distribution of work units (*tasks*) by exchanging messages among the machines that are interconnected as a network, or local workers. A task is the key concept in Celery; any sort of job we must distribute has to be encapsulated in a task beforehand.

Why use Celery?

We could justify the use of Celery by listing some of its positive points:

- It distributes tasks in a transparent way among workers that are spread over the Internet, or local workers
- It changes, in a simple way, the concurrence of workers through setup (*processes, threads, Gevent, Eventlet*)
- It supports synchronous, asynchronous, periodic, and scheduled tasks
- It re-executes tasks in case of errors

 It is common for some developers to claim that synchronous tasks are the same as real-time tasks. This is an unnecessary confusion as the concepts are totally different. For a real-time task, we should understand that the task has a window of time in which it has to be executed. In case it does not happen, then this task will be aborted or paused for further execution, while a synchronous task returns the result when it's done.

Understanding Celery's architecture

Celery has an architecture based on *pluggable* components and a mechanism of message exchange that uses a protocol according to a selected *message transport* (*broker*). This is illustrated in the following diagram:

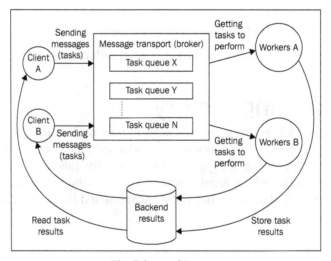

The Celery architecture

Now, let us go through each item within Celery's architecture in detail.

Working with tasks

The *client* components, as presented in the previous diagram, have the function of creating and dispatching tasks to the brokers.

We will now analyze a code example that demonstrates the definition of a task by using the `@app.task` decorator, which is accessible through an instance of Celery application that, for now, will be called `app`. The following code example demonstrates a simple `Hello World` app:

```
@app.task
def hello_world():
    return "Hello I'm a celery task"
```

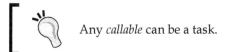 Any *callable* can be a task.

As we mentioned earlier, there are several types of tasks: synchronous, asynchronous, periodic, and scheduled. When we perform a task call, it returns an instance of type `AsyncResult`. The `AsyncResult` object is an object that allows the task status to be checked, its ending, and obviously, its return when it exists. However, to make use of this mechanism, another component, the *result backend*, has to be active. This will be explained further in this chapter. To dispatch a task, we should make use of some of the following methods of the task:

- `delay(arg, kwarg=value)`: This is a shortcut to call the `apply_async` method.
- `apply_async((arg,), {'kwarg': value})`: This allows the setting up of a series of interesting parameters for the execution of the task. Some of them are as follows:
  - `countdown`: This represents the number of seconds available in the future so that the task execution is started. The default task is executed immediately.
  - `expires`: This represents the period of time or date after which a certain task will no longer be executed.
  - `retry`: In the case of a failure in the connection or sending of a task, this parameter has to be resent.
  - `queue`: This is a line to which the task has to be referred.

- ○ `serializer`: This represents a data format for the serialization of tasks in disk, and some examples include `json`, `yaml`, and others.

- ○ `link`: This links one or more tasks to be executed in case the sent task is executed successfully.

- ○ `link_error`: This links one or more tasks to be executed in the case of a failure in the execution of the task.

- `apply((arg,), {'kwarg': value})`: This executes a task in the local process in a synchronous way, thereby blocking up to the point a result is ready.

> Celery also provides mechanisms to accompany the status of a task, which is quite useful to track and map the real status of processing. More information about the task status built-in is available at `http://celery.readthedocs.org/en/latest/reference/celery.states.html`.

Discovering message transport (broker)

A *broker* is definitely a key component in Celery. Through it, we get to send and receive messages and communicate with workers. Celery supports a large number of brokers. However, to some of these, not all Celery mechanisms are implemented. The most complete in terms of functionality are **RabbitMQ** and **Redis**. In this book, we will use Redis as a broker as well as result backend. A broker has the function of providing a means of communication between client applications that send tasks and workers that will execute them. This is done by using task queues. We can have several network machines with brokers waiting to receive messages to be consumed by workers.

Understanding workers

Workers are responsible for executing the tasks they have received. Celery displays a series of mechanisms so that we can find the best way to control how workers will behave. We can define the mechanisms as follows:

- **Concurrency mode**: This is the mode with which workers will perform, for instance, processes, threads, Eventlet, and Gevent

- **Remote control**: Using this mechanism, we can send messages directly to a specific worker or a list of them through a high priority queue aiming to alter their behavior, including runtime

- **Revoking tasks**: Using this mechanism, we can instruct one or more workers to ignore the execution of one or more tasks

Many more features can be set up and even altered in runtime if necessary. For instance, the number of tasks a worker executes per period of time, from which queue the workers will consume the most time, and and so on. More information about workers is available at `http://docs.celeryproject.org/en/latest/userguide/workers.html#remote-control`.

Understanding result backends

The result backend component has the role of storing the status and result of the task to return to the client application. From the result backend supported by Celery, we can highlight *RabbitMQ*, *Redis*, *MongoDB*, *Memcached*, among others. Each result backend listed previously has strong and weak points. Refer to `http://docs.celeryproject.org/en/latest/userguide/tasks.html#task-result-backends` for further information.

Now, we have a general idea of the Celery architecture and its components. So, let us set up a developing environment that will be used to implement our case studies.

Setting up the environment

In this section, we will set up two machines in Linux. The first one, hostname `foshan`, will perform the client role, where app Celery will dispatch the tasks to be executed. The other machine, hostname *Phoenix,* will perform the role of a broker, result backend, and the queues consumed by workers.

Setting up the client machine

Let us start the setup of the client machine. In this machine, we will set up a virtual environment with Python 3.3, using the tool `pyvenv`. The goal of `pyvenv` is to not pollute Python present in the operating system with additional modules, but to separate the developing environments necessary for each project. We will execute the following command to create our virtual environment:

```
$pyvenv celery_env
```

The preceding line creates a directory called `celery_env` in the current path, which contains all the structures necessary to isolate the developing environment in Python. The following screenshot illustrates the structure created in the `celery_env` directory:

```
:: ~ yipman@foshan: ~/documents/parallel_programming_with_python/celery_env
yipman@foshan:~/documents/parallel_programming_with_python/celery_env$ ls
bin  include  lib  pyvenv.cfg
yipman@foshan:~/documents/parallel_programming_with_python/celery_env$ 
```

Structure of a virtual Python environment

After the creation of this virtual environment, we can start our work and install the packages to be used. However, first of all, we need to activate it. For this, we will execute the following command from the root of `celery_env`:

`$source bin/activate`

A change in the prompt of the command, such as `celery_env` on the left of the prompt, which will indicate that they are now in an activated environment. All you do in terms of installing packages and Python will result in changes in this directory but not in the system.

> Using a `--system-site-packages` flag, we can create virtual environments that have access to site-packages present in Python that is installed in the system. However, this is not recommended.

Now, we have a virtual environment and starting off from the point from where you already installed `setuptools` or `pip`, we will install the necessary packages for our client. Let's install the Celery framework with the following command:

`$pip install celery`

The following screenshot shows the installed framework v3.1.9, which will be used in this book:

```
Python 3.3.5 (default, Mar 13 2014, 16:33:47)
[GCC 4.7.2] on linux
Type "help", "copyright", "credits" or "license" for more information.
>>> import celery
>>> celery.VERSION
version_info_t(major=3, minor=1, micro=9, releaselevel='', serial='')
>>> 
```

The Celery framework

Now, we need to install the support to Redis in our Celery so that our Client transmits messages through our broker. We use the following command for this purpose:

```
$pip install celery[redis]
```

We have now got the infrastructure of our client completed. Before coding, we must set up our server where the brokers and workers will remain.

Setting up the server machine

To set up the server machine, we will start by installing Redis, which will be our broker and result backend. We will do this using the following command:

```
$sudo apt-get install redis-server
```

To start Redis, just execute the following command:

```
$redis-server
```

If it was successful, an output similar to the following screenshot will be exhibited:

```
iceman@phoenix:~/8397_07_broker$ redis-server
[5834] 16 Mar 21:55:39 # Warning: no config file specified, using the default config
o/redis.conf'
[5834] 16 Mar 21:55:39 * Server started, Redis version 2.2.12
[5834] 16 Mar 21:55:39 # WARNING overcommit_memory is set to 0! Background save may
ercommit_memory = 1' to /etc/sysctl.conf and then reboot or run the command 'sysctl
[5834] 16 Mar 21:55:39 * DB loaded from disk: 0 seconds
[5834] 16 Mar 21:55:39 * The server is now ready to accept connections on port 6379
[5834] 16 Mar 21:55:39 - 0 clients connected (0 slaves), 790592 bytes in use
```

Redis server running

Dispatching a simple task

At this point, we have a ready environment. Let's test it by sending a task that will calculate the square root of a value and return a result.

First, we must define our task module `tasks.py` inside the server. Let's check the description of the `tasks.py` module. In the following chunk of code, we have imports necessary for our function that will calculate the square root:

```
from math import sqrt
from celery import Celery
```

Now, let's create the following instance of Celery, which will represent our client application:

```
app = Celery('tasks', broker='redis://192.168.25.21:6379/0')
```

We have created an instance of Celery that will control some aspects of our application. Notice that in its initializer, we informed the name of the module in which definitions of the task are present and we stated the address of the broker as a second argument.

Then, we have to set up our result backend, which will also be in Redis, as follows:

```
app.config.CELERY_RESULT_BACKEND = 'redis://192.168.25.21:6379/0'
```

With the basics ready, let's define our task with the `@app.task` decorator:

```
@app.task
def square_root(value):
    return sqrt(value)
```

At this point, since we have our `tasks.py` module defined, we need to initiate our workers inside the server, where Redis and Celery (with support to Redis) are installed. For this, we have created a separated directory to keep it organized; we will call it `8397_07_broker`. We will copy our `tasks.py` module inside this directory and run the following command from it:

$celery –A tasks worker --loglevel=INFO

The preceding command initiates a Celery server, and by means of the `-A` parameter informs where the instance of application Celery is defined, and the implementation of the tasks. The following screenshot shows part of the Celery application initialized beside the server:

```
(8397_07_broker) iceman@phoenix:~/8397_07_broker$ celery -A tasks worker --loglevel=info

 -------------- celery@phoenix v3.1.9 (Cipater)
---- **** -----
--- * ***  * -- Linux-3.8.0-37-generic-x86_64-with-debian-wheezy-sid
-- * - **** ---
- ** ---------- [config]
- ** ---------- .> app:         tasks:0x7f318a8c2d50
- ** ---------- .> transport:   redis://192.168.25.21:6379/0
- ** ---------- .> results:     redis://192.168.25.21:6379/0
- *** --- * --- .> concurrency: 4 (prefork)
-- ******* ----
--- ***** ----- [queues]
 -------------- .> celery            exchange=celery(direct) key=celery


[tasks]
  . tasks.sqrt_task

[2014-03-17 16:06:34,867: INFO/MainProcess] Connected to redis://192.168.25.21:6379/0
[2014-03-17 16:06:34,880: INFO/MainProcess] mingle: searching for neighbors
[2014-03-17 16:06:35,894: INFO/MainProcess] mingle: all alone
[2014-03-17 16:06:35,914: WARNING/MainProcess] celery@phoenix ready.
```

Celery server side started

Now, we have a Celery server waiting to receive tasks and send them to workers. The next step is to create an application on the client side to call tasks.

 It is important not to skip this stage as the following sections will make use of the structure created previously.

In the machine that represents the client, we have our virtual environment `celery_env` already set up, remember? So, now it is simpler to create a step-by-step module `task_dispatcher.py`, as follows:

1. We import the `logging` module to exhibit information referring to the execution of the program and the `Celery` class inside the `celery` module, as follows:

```
import logging
from celery import Celery
```

2. The next step is to create an instance of the `Celery` class informing the module containing the tasks and then the broker, as done in the server side. This is done with the following code:

```
#logger configuration...
app = Celery('tasks',
  broker='redis://192.168.25.21:6379/0')
app.conf.CELERY_RESULT_BACKEND =
  'redis://192.168.25.21:6397/0'
```

 A result backend was supposed to be set up directly on the initialization of a Celery instance; however, the setup was ignored by the framework during the experiment.

There are more elegant ways of setting up a Celery app — by creating a Python module and inserting it in the command line. We will do it directly in the code to keep the simplicity of the examples.

As we are going to reuse this module to implement calls to tasks in future sections of this chapter, let us create a function to encapsulate the sending of the `sqrt_task(value)` task. We will create the `manage_sqrt_task(value)` function as follows:

```
def manage_sqrt_task(value):
    result = app.send_task('tasks.sqrt_task', args=(value,))
    logging.info(result.get())
```

We can notice in the preceding chunk that the client application does not need to recognize the implementation of the side server. By means of send_task that is inside the Celery class, we can invoke tasks only by informing a string in the <module.task> format and passing arguments in tuple format. Finally, we exhibit the result in the log.

In the __main__ block, we executed the call to the manage_sqrt_task(value) function by passing the input value as 4:

```
if __name__ == '__main__':
    manage_sqrt_task(4)
```

The following screenshot shows the result of the execution of file task_dispatcher.py:

```
INFO/MainProcess] Received task: tasks.sqrt_task[54b604c6-93fb-49f2-be55-0f0891a04252]
INFO/MainProcess] Task tasks.sqrt_task[54b604c6-93fb-49f2-be55-0f0891a04252] succeeded in 0.
```

sqrt_task in the Celery server

In client side, the result is obtained through a call to the get() method, which is featured in the AsyncResult instance returned by send_task(). We can check the result in the following screenshot:

```
(celery_env) yipman@foshan:~/Documents/parallel_programming_with_python/celery_env$ python task_dispatcher.py
2014-03-20 13:17:22,587 - 2.0
```

sqrt_task result in client side

Using Celery to obtain a Fibonacci series term

Let us again go and distribute our multiple inputs in order to calculate the *n*th Fibonacci term, each of them in a distributed way. The function that calculates Fibonacci will change a little in relation to the previous chapters. The changes are small; now we have the @app.task decorator and a small change in the return message.

In the tasks.py module (created previously), which is in the server machine where also the broker is, we will stop the execution of Celery (*Ctrl* + *C*) and add the fibo_task task. This is done by using the following code:

```
@app.task
def fibo_task(value):
    a, b = 0,1
    for item in range(value):
```

```
    a, b = b, a + b
message = "The Fibonacci calculated with task id %s" \
    " was %d" % (fibo_task.request.id, a)
Return (value, message)
```

A point to observe is that we obtain the ID of the task with the `<task.request.id>` call. The `request` object is an object in the `task` class, which provides a context to the execution of the task. The context gives us information, for instance, the ID of the task.

After adding the new task to the `tasks.py` module, let us initiate Celery again and the result is shown in the following screenshot:

```
- ** ---------- [config]
- ** ---------- .> app:           tasks:0x7f68de79ff10
- ** ---------- .> transport:     redis://192.168.25.21:6379/0
- ** ---------- .> results:       redis://192.168.25.21:6379/0
- *** --- * --- .> concurrency: 4 (prefork)
-- ******* ----
--- ***** ----- [queues]
------------- .> celery                 exchange=celery(direct) key=celery


[tasks]
  . tasks.fibo_task
  . tasks.sqrt_task
```

fibo_task loaded

Now that we have our `fibo_task` task loaded in the Celery server, we will implement the call to this function in the client side.

In the `task_dispatcher.py` module featured in the client machine, we will declare our `input_list` in order to test it, as follows:

```
input_list = [4, 3, 8, 6, 10]
```

As we did in the `sqrt_task` task created in the previous section, we will create a method to organize our calls without polluting the __main__ block. We will name this function `manage_fibo_task`. Check out the following implementation:

```
def manage_fibo_task(value_list):
    async_result_dict = {x: app.send_task('tasks.fibo_task',
        args=(x,)) for x in value_list}

    for key, value in async_result_dict.items():
        logger.info("Value [%d] -> %s" % (key, value.get()[1]))
```

In the `manage_fibo_task` function, we created a dictionary called `async_result_dict`, populating the same pair of key values. `key` is the item passed as an argument to obtain the umpteenth term of Fibonacci and `value` is the instance of AsyncResult returned from the call to the `send_task` method. With this method, we can monitor the status and result of a task.

Finally, we iterated the dictionary exhibiting the input values and their respective umpteenth obtained terms of Fibonacci. The `get()` function of the `AsyncResult` class allows us to obtain the processing results.

It is possible to notice that the `get()` function might not return an immediate result as the processing will still be taking place. A call to the `get()` method in the client side can block the processing that comes after the call. It is a good idea to unite the call to the `ready()` method, permitting to check whether a result is ready to be obtained.

So, our result exhibition loop could be something similar to the following code:

```
for key, value in async_result_dict.items():
    if value.ready():
        logger.info("Value [%d] -> %s" % (key,
            value.get()[1]))
    else:
        logger.info("Task [%s] is not ready" % value.task_id)
```

Depending on the type of task to be executed, there may be a considerable delay in the result. Therefore, by calling `get()` without considering the return status, we can block the code running at the point where the `get()` function was called. To tackle this, we should define an argument called `timeout` in the `get(timeout=x)` method. So, by minimizing this blocking, we can prevent tasks from having problems in returning results, which would impact the running of the execution for an indefinite time.

Finally, we added a call to the `manage_fibo_task` function, passing as argument to our `input_list`. The code is as follows:

```
if __name__ == '__main__':
    #manage_sqrt_task(4)
    manage_fibo_task(input_list)
```

When we execute the code in `task_dispatcher.py`, the following output server can be visualized in the side:

```
[2014-03-20 16:31:29,448: INFO/MainProcess] Received task: tasks.fibo_task[8e1820ef-bb5a-47ca-8bdf-db06b59c53e1]
[2014-03-20 16:31:29,453: INFO/MainProcess] Task tasks.fibo_task[8e1820ef-bb5a-47ca-8bdf-db06b59c53e1] succeeded in 0.
0020779879996553063s: (4, 'The fibonacci calculated by worker 8e1820ef-bb5a-47ca-8bdf-db06b59c53e1 was 3')
[2014-03-20 16:31:29,456: INFO/MainProcess] Received task: tasks.fibo_task[04d61475-164f-49b1-bca1-748a5317d23e]
[2014-03-20 16:31:29,460: INFO/MainProcess] Task tasks.fibo_task[04d61475-164f-49b1-bca1-748a5317d23e] succeeded in 0.
0022077469620853662s: (3, 'The fibonacci calculated by worker 04d61475-164f-49b1-bca1-748a5317d23e was 2')
[2014-03-20 16:31:29,463: INFO/MainProcess] Received task: tasks.fibo_task[ae7b47c2-4c89-4bd9-b25d-6f38fe2b3b0a]
[2014-03-20 16:31:29,469: INFO/MainProcess] Task tasks.fibo_task[ae7b47c2-4c89-4bd9-b25d-6f38fe2b3b0a] succeeded in 0.
0027012709761038423s: (8, 'The fibonacci calculated by worker ae7b47c2-4c89-4bd9-b25d-6f38fe2b3b0a was 21')
[2014-03-20 16:31:29,471: INFO/MainProcess] Received task: tasks.fibo_task[498033e5-5758-41c9-827a-83dc55a8de70]
[2014-03-20 16:31:29,475: INFO/MainProcess] Task tasks.fibo_task[498033e5-5758-41c9-827a-83dc55a8de70] succeeded in 0.
0019668620079755783s: (6, 'The fibonacci calculated by worker 498033e5-5758-41c9-827a-83dc55a8de70 was 8')
[2014-03-20 16:31:29,485: INFO/MainProcess] Received task: tasks.fibo_task[455f9638-e49d-4a1a-84a1-5331bf680d6e]
[2014-03-20 16:31:29,489: INFO/MainProcess] Task tasks.fibo_task[455f9638-e49d-4a1a-84a1-5331bf680d6e] succeeded in 0.
0019953069859184325s: (10, 'The fibonacci calculated by worker 455f9638-e49d-4a1a-84a1-5331bf680d6e was 55')
```

The server side for fibo_task

In the client side, we have the following output:

```
(celery_env) yipman@foshan:~/Documents/parallel_programming_with_python/celery_env$ python task_dispatcher.py
2014-03-20 16:31:08,390 - Value [8] -> The fibonacci calculated by worker 6a47e7b2-cdff-4ba0-981d-29bf71bf4096 was 21
2014-03-20 16:31:08,393 - Value [10] -> The fibonacci calculated by worker cdcaff99-677b-42d5-b591-ec6a0dce24ca was 55
2014-03-20 16:31:08,397 - Value [3] -> The fibonacci calculated by worker 71d47e08-71e8-4559-a209-f8c17c06ecaa was 2
2014-03-20 16:31:08,401 - Value [4] -> The fibonacci calculated by worker 6f73ca3e-76f1-4a25-b6b0-102bb6d724ea was 3
2014-03-20 16:31:08,404 - Value [6] -> The fibonacci calculated by worker c1f11463-18b0-45d9-b0eb-ef47868702ed was 8
```

The client side for fibo_task

Defining queues by task types

The task that is responsible for calculating Fibonacci was implemented and is running. We can see that all tasks are being sent to a default queue of Celery. However, there are ways to route a task to different queues; let us refactor our architecture in server side and implement what is known as routing task from the client side. We will specify queues for each type of task.

At the moment we start the Celery server in the server side, we will establish three different queues. These will now be seen and consumed by the workers. The queues are `fibo_queue` for Fibonacci tasks, `sqrt_queue` for square root tasks, and `webcrawler_queue` for the Web crawler ones. However, what is the advantage of having task fluxes separated? Let's observe them as follows:

- It groups tasks of the same type to make their monitoring easier
- It defines workers dedicated to consume a specific queue, thereby enhancing performance
- It distributes queues with heavier tasks to brokers allocated in machines with better performance

> The preceding points are not going to be explained in this book, but we can make a load balance by initializing the Celery servers and even distributing brokers with dedicated queues in a network. I recommend that you try this cluster style using Celery.

To set up the queues in the server, we only need to initiate Celery with the following command:

```
$celery -A tasks -Q sqrt_queue,fibo_queue,webcrawler_queue worker
--loglevel=info
```

The following screenshot shows the active files in server:

```
[queues]
.> fibo_queue        exchange=fibo_queue(direct) key=fibo_queue
.> sqrt_queue        exchange=sqrt_queue(direct) key=sqrt_queue
.> webcrawler_queue exchange=webcrawler_queue(direct) key=webcrawler_queue
```

Different queues in the Celery server

Before moving to the next example, let us route the sending of the existing tasks to their queues. In the server side, in the `task_dispatcher.py` module, we will alter the `send_task` calls so that the next time the tasks are dispatched, they will be directed to distinct queues. We will now alter the `sqrt_task` call as follows:

```
app.send_task('tasks.sqrt_task', args=(value,),
    queue='sqrt_queue', routing_key='sqrt_queue')
```

Then, we will alter the `fibo_task` call as follows:

```
app.send_task('tasks.fibo_task', args=(x,), queue='fibo_queue',
    routing_key='fibo_queue')
```

> If you have an interest in monitoring queues, checking the quantity of tasks addressed to them, and other things, the Celery documentation provides a great deal of information at http://celery.readthedocs.org/en/latest/userguide/monitoring.html.
>
> In any case, while using Redis, its own utility `redis-cli` can be a tool.
>
> As queues and tasks, workers can also be monitored and adjusted. More information is available at http://celery.readthedocs.org/en/latest/userguide/monitoring.html#workers.

Using Celery to make a distributed Web crawler

We will now move on to adapting our Web crawler to Celery. We already have `webcrawler_queue`, which is responsible for encapsulating web-type `hcrawler` tasks. However, in the server side, we will create our `crawl_task` task inside the `tasks.py` module.

First, we will add our imports to the `re` and `requests` modules, which are the modules for regular expression and the HTTP library respectively. The code is as follows:

```
import re
import requests
```

Then, we will define our regular expression, which we studied in the previous chapters, as follows:

```
hTML_link_regex = re.compile(
    '<a\s(?:.*?\s)*?href=[\'"](.*?)[\'"].*?>')
```

Now, we will place our `crawl_task` function in the Web crawler, add the `@app.task` decorator, and change the return message a bit, as follows:

```
@app.task
def crawl_task(url):
    request_data = requests.get(url)
    links = html_link_regex.findall(request_data.text)
    message = "The task %s found the following links %s.."\
    Return message
```

Notice that the list of links found won't necessarily match the following screenshot:

```
[tasks]
  . tasks.crawl_task
  . tasks.fibo_task
  . tasks.sqrt_task
```

crawl_task added to the Celery server

Let's then scroll up Celery again and see. At this point, with our new task loaded, it is time to implement the task called `crawl_task` in the client side in the `task_dispatcher.py` module.

First, we need a list of links that will be our data input; we will call it `url_list`. The code to do this is as follows:

```
url_list = ['http://www.google.com',
            'http://br.bing.com',
            'http://duckduckgo.com',
            'http://github.com',
            'http://br.search.yahoo.com']
```

We will create, as we did in other tasks, a `manage_crawl_task` function containing the logic of the `crawl_task` call in order to organize the __main__ block. The code is as follows:

```
def manage_crawl_task(url_list):
    async_result_dict = {url: app.send_task('tasks.crawl_task',
args=(url,), queue='webcrawler_queue',
routing_key='webcrawler_queue') for url in url_list}

    for key, value in async_result_dict.items():
        if value.ready():
            logger.info("%s -> %s" % (key, value.get()))
        else:
            logger.info("The task [%s] is not ready" %
value.task_id)
```

As in `manage_fibo_task` we have created in the previous function, a dictionary containing the current URL as key, and an object (`AsyncResult`) as a value is passed to the function. After that, we checked the task status and have taken the result to the tasks that are concluded.

Now, we can insert the call of the function in the __main__ block to test its functioning. The code is as follows:

```
if __main__ == '__main__':
    #manage_sqrt_task(4)
    #manage_fibo_task(input_list)
    manage_crawl_task(url_list)
```

While running our `task_dispatcher.py` code, we have the following output on the server side:

```
[2014-03-22 01:49:31,742: INFO/MainProcess] Received task: tasks.crawl_task[3c395046-87d2-4829-b257-ab3ebbc22db2]
[2014-03-22 01:49:31,751: INFO/MainProcess] Received task: tasks.crawl_task[ee9f7593-f156-441a-a80b-ccedb82d905a]
[2014-03-22 01:49:31,752: INFO/Worker-3] Starting new HTTP connection (1): www.google.com
[2014-03-22 01:49:31,756: INFO/MainProcess] Received task: tasks.crawl_task[fe69611a-105c-487e-9177-05511ba26901]
[2014-03-22 01:49:31,757: INFO/Worker-4] Starting new HTTP connection (1): br.bing.com
[2014-03-22 01:49:31,760: INFO/Worker-1] Starting new HTTP connection (1): duckduckgo.com
[2014-03-22 01:49:31,768: INFO/MainProcess] Received task: tasks.crawl_task[22f07565-a0e2-487e-9132-ea1ceadc22a9]
[2014-03-22 01:49:31,775: INFO/MainProcess] Received task: tasks.crawl_task[968640e2-6480-43b4-a18e-bdfc5243e717]
[2014-03-22 01:49:32,061: INFO/Worker-3] Starting new HTTP connection (1): www.google.com.br
[2014-03-22 01:49:32,099: INFO/Worker-4] Starting new HTTP connection (1): www.bing.com
[2014-03-22 01:49:32,223: INFO/Worker-1] Starting new HTTPS connection (1): duckduckgo.com
[2014-03-22 01:49:32,394: INFO/MainProcess] Task tasks.crawl_task[3c395046-87d2-4829-b257-ab3ebbc22db2] succeeded in 0
.6491261390001455s: "The task 3c395046-87d2-4829-b257-ab3ebbc22db2 found the following links ['http://www.google.com.b
/imghp?hl=pt-BR&tab=wi',...
[2014-03-22 01:49:32,395: INFO/Worker-3] Starting new HTTP connection (1): github.com
[2014-03-22 01:49:32,477: INFO/MainProcess] Task tasks.crawl_task[ee9f7593-f156-441a-a80b-ccedb82d905a] succeeded in 0
.7225970590006909s: "The task ee9f7593-f156-441a-a80b-ccedb82d905a found the following links ['/account/web?sh=5&amp;r
u=%2f',...
[2014-03-22 01:49:32,815: INFO/Worker-3] Starting new HTTPS connection (1): github.com
[2014-03-22 01:49:32,975: INFO/MainProcess] Task tasks.crawl_task[fe69611a-105c-487e-9177-05511ba26901] succeeded in 1
.2173123520005902s: "The task fe69611a-105c-487e-9177-05511ba26901 found the following links ['/about', '/Internationa
l_Women'].. "
[2014-03-22 01:49:33,531: INFO/MainProcess] Task tasks.crawl_task[22f07565-a0e2-487e-9132-ea1ceadc22a9] succeeded in 1
.1373520119996101s: "The task 22f07565-a0e2-487e-9132-ea1ceadc22a9 found the following links ['#start-of-content', 'ht
tps://github.com/'].. "
[2014-03-22 01:49:33,533: INFO/Worker-3] Starting new HTTP connection (1): br.search.yahoo.com
[2014-03-22 01:49:34,080: INFO/MainProcess] Task tasks.crawl_task[968640e2-6480-43b4-a18e-bdfc5243e717] succeeded in 0
.5486545060011849s: "The task 968640e2-6480-43b4-a18e-bdfc5243e717 found the following links ['http://br.yahoo.com/',.
```

crawl_task on the server side

Finally, we have the execution output in the client side, as shown in the following screenshot:

```
(celery_env)iceman@iceman-Q470C-500P4C:~/Documents/parallel_programming_with_python/celery_env$ python task_dispatcher.py
http://br.search.yahoo.com -> The task d2eaa01d-2411-4aff-a457-6606a43d122f found the following links ['https://br.yahoo.com/',
l.yahoo.com/']..
http://duckduckgo.com -> The task 4b9c448f-b6d5-4dd3-8e96-01a35c4bac62 found the following links ['javascript:;', '#']..
http://github.com -> The task 07d5a3c3-6d0b-4d0f-b321-635bc61611c3 found the following links ['#start-of-content', 'https://githu
http://www.google.com -> The task 2f28ac81-a761-4446-add6-87e1466b84f7 found the following links ['http://www.google.com.br/imghp
wi', 'http://maps.google.com/maps?hl=pt-BR&tab=wl']..
http://br.bing.com -> The task d658fcc3-4fbf-40eb-9814-f7aec01f5b57 found the following links ['/account/web?sh=5&amp;ru=%2f', '
;FORM=Z9LH']..
```

crawl_task on the client side

Celery is a great tool that offers a good range of resources. We explored the basic resources that we consider necessary for this chapter. Yet, there is a lot more to explore and we recommend that you experiment with it in a real-life project.

Summary

In this chapter, we discussed the Celery distributed task queue. We also visualized its architecture, analyzed its key components, and saw how to set up an environment to build basic applications with Celery. It is possible to write a book only about Celery, and I hope that I have been fair and just while choosing the topics throughout.

In the next chapter, we will study the `asyncio` module as well as learn how to execute processing in an asynchronous way. We will also have a brief introduction to `coroutines`, and learn how to use them with `asyncio`.

8
Doing Things Asynchronously

In the previous chapter, we learned how to distribute tasks using the Celery framework and parallelize computing in different machines linked by a network. Now, we are going to explore asynchronous programming, event loop, and coroutines, which are resources featured in the `asyncio` module available in Python Version 3.4. We are also going to learn to make use of those in combination with executors.

In this chapter, we will cover:

- Blocking, nonblocking, and asynchronous operations
- Understanding event loop
- Using `asyncio`

Understanding blocking, nonblocking, and asynchronous operations

Understanding the different approaches to task execution is extremely important to model and conceive a scalable solution. Knowing when to use asynchronous, blocking, and nonblocking operations can make an enormous difference in the response time of a system.

Understanding blocking operations

In the case of a blocking operation, we can use the example of attending a customer at a bank counter. When the customer's number is called for attendance, all the attention of the cashier is focused on this specific customer. Until the necessity of the current customer is achieved, the cashier can't attend another customer simultaneously. Now, with this in mind, imagine a bank agency with only two cashiers and an influx of 100 customers per hour; we have then a flow problem. This case illustrates the blocking of processing, when a task needs to wait for another to end, blocking the access to resources.

> In the blocking of processing, the solicitor blocks the result until its solicitation is fulfilled.

Understanding nonblocking operations

It is easy to confuse nonblocking operations with asynchronous operations; however, they are different concepts that work really well in unison being often used this way. Let us again use a real-world scenery to illustrate this situation. Back to the bank environment, imagine that among the clients waiting to be attended, there is a client X who needs to withdraw a benefit, but benefits are not available at the moment. The cashier, instead of blocking the attendance to other clients until the benefit withdrawal is available, simply signalizes to client X to return at another moment or another date.

> A non-blocking operator is one that, at a minimal blocking sign, returns a control code or exception that tells the solicitor to retry later.

Understanding asynchronous operations

Back to the bank agency example, imagine that each cashier has 10 assistants to execute tasks that take longer; now consider our agency has two cashiers, each one with 10 assistants. As clients arrive, if client X has a solicitation that could block the queue for an unlimited amount of time, this solicitation is dispatched to an assistant that will do the job in the background and will approach the client X directly when his or her answer is ready, thus freeing the cashier to process the request from the following client without having to wait for the previous accomplishment.

Asynchronous operations notify the end of solicitations by means of callbacks, coroutines, and other mechanisms.

A **callback** function is a function that is called when a certain condition occurs. It is commonly used to handle results from asynchronous processing.

Understanding event loop

In order to understand the concept of event loop, we need to understand the elements that form its inner structure.

We will use the term **resource descriptor** to refer to the socket descriptor as well as file descriptor.

Polling functions

The polling technique is implemented by different operating systems aiming to monitor the status of one or more resource descriptors. Systems implement this technique by means of functions. Polling functions form the basis of event loops. We can often find these models being referred to as **readiness** notification scheme due to the fact that the polling function notifies the one interested in the event, that the resource descriptor is ready for interaction; the one interested, however, might/might not accomplish the desired operation.

In terms of Linux, for instance, we have the following polling functions:

- `select()`: This POSIX implementation presents some disadvantages, which are as follows:
    - Limitation in the number of resource descriptors to be monitored
    - Complexity O(n), where n represents the number of connected clients, which makes it unviable for servers to attend multiple clients simultaneously

- `poll()`: This is an enhancement in response to `select()`, with the following features:
    - Allows a larger range of resource descriptors to be monitored
    - Complexity O(n) as `select()`
    - Allows a larger variety of types of monitored events
    - Reuses entry data in its call, in contrast to `select()`

- `epoll()`: This is a powerful implementation to Linux and has the attractive feature of constant complexity O(1). The `epoll()` function offers two behaviors to monitor events through the `epoll_wait()` call (http://refspecs.linux-foundation.org/LSB_4.0.0/LSB-Core-generic/LSB-Core-generic/libc-epoll-wait-1.html). To define these two behaviors, let's imagine a scenery where we have a producer writing data in a socket (that has an associated socket descriptor) and a consumer waiting to accomplish the reading of data:

  - **Level-triggered**: When the consumer accomplishes a call to `epoll_wait()`, it will get the status of that resource descriptor immediately returned to the solicited event, indicating the possibility (or not) of executing the reading operation (in our case). So, level-triggered behavior is directly related to the status of the event and not the event itself.

  - **Edge-triggered**: A call to `epoll_wait()` will return only when the writing event in the socket is concluded and data is available. So, in edge-triggered behavior the focus is the event itself having taken place and not the possibility of executing any event.

> On other platforms, there are also polling functions available, such as **kqueue** for BSD and Mac OS X.
>
> Polling functions are useful to create applications with a single thread that can manage multiple operations in concurrent way. Tornado web server (http://www.tornadoweb.org/en/stable/overview.html), for example, was written using non-blocking I/O, and as a polling function, it supports `epoll` and `kqueue` for Linux and BSD/Mac OS X, respectively.

Polling functions work in the following steps:

1. A `poller` object is created.

2. We can register or not one or more resource descriptors in `poller`.

3. The polling function is executed in the created `poller` object.

> Poller is an interface that provides abstraction to the use of polling functions.

Using event loops

We can define event loops as abstractions that ease up using polling functions to monitor events. Internally, event loops make use of poller objects, taking away the responsibility of the programmer to control the tasks of addition, removal, and control of events.

Loops of events, in general, make use of callback functions to treat the occurrence of an event; for example, given a resource descriptor A, when a writing event happens in A, there will be a callback function for it. Some examples of applications that implement event loop in Python are listed as follows:

- Tornado web server (http://www.tornadoweb.org/en/stable/): This has a strong point—it uses epoll as the polling function if the environment is Linux and has kqueue support in case of BSD or Mac OS X

- Twisted (https://twistedmatrix.com/trac/): This is a popular framework of Python applications and offers an implementation of the event loop

- asyncio (https://docs.python.org/3.4/library/asyncio.html): This module written by Guido Van Rossum, among others, offers an implementation of an event loop. It is featured in Python 3.4

- Gevent (http://www.gevent.org/): This provides an event loop based on libev

- Eventlet (https://pypi.python.org/pypi/eventlet): This implements an event loop based on libevent

Using asyncio

We can define asyncio as a module that came to reboot asynchronous programming in Python. The asyncio module allows the implementation of asynchronous programming using a combination of the following elements:

- **Event loop**: This was already defined in the previous section. The asyncio module allows an event loop per process.

- **Coroutines**: As mentioned in the official documentation of asyncio, "A coroutine is a generator that follows certain conventions." Its most interesting feature is that it can be suspended during execution to wait for external processing (some routine in I/O) and return from the point it had stopped when the external processing is done.

- **Futures**: The `asyncio` module defines its own object Future. Futures represent a processing that has still not been accomplished.

- **Tasks**: This is a subclass of `asyncio.Future` to encapsulate and manage coroutines.

Beyond these mechanisms, `asyncio` provides a series of other features for the developing of applications, such as transports and protocols, which allow communication by means of channels using TCP, SSL, UDP, and pipes, among other things. More information on `asyncio` is available at `https://docs.python.org/3.4/library/asyncio.html`.

Understanding coroutines and futures

To be able to define a coroutine in `asyncio`, we use the `@asyncio.coroutine` decorator, and we must make use of the `yield from` syntax to suspend the coroutine in order to execute an operation I/O or another computing that might block the event loop where the coroutine will execute. But how does this mechanism of suspension and resumption work? Coroutines work together with the `asyncio.Future` objects. We can summarize the operation as follows:

- Coroutine is initialized, and an `asyncio.Future` object is instanced internally or passed as an argument to coroutine.

- On reaching the point of the coroutine where there is use of `yield from`, the coroutine is then suspended to wait for computing evoked in `yield from`. The `yield from` instance waits for the `yield from <coroutine or asyncio.Future or asyncio.Task>` construction.

- When the evoked computing in `yield from` ends, the coroutine executes the `set_result(<result>)` method of the `asyncio.Future` object related to the coroutine, telling the event loop that coroutine can be resumed.

 When we use the `asyncio.Task` object to encapsulate a coroutine, we do not need to explicit the use of a `asyncio.Future` object, as the `asyncio.Task` object is already a subclass of `asyncio.Future`.

Using coroutine and asyncio.Future

Let us verify some example code using coroutine and the `asyncio.Future` object:

```
import asyncio

@asyncio.coroutine
```

```
def sleep_coroutine(f):
    yield from asyncio.sleep(2)
    f.set_result("Done!")
```

In the preceding chunk, we defined our coroutine named `sleep_coroutine`, which receives an object `asyncio.Future` as an argument. In the sequence, our coroutine will be suspended for the execution of `asyncio.sleep(2)`, which will sleep for 2 seconds; we must observe that the `asyncio.sleep` function is already compatible with `asyncio`. Therefore, it returns as future; however, due to didactic reasons, we included our `asyncio.Future` object passed as an argument to illustrate how the resumption could be done in a coroutine explicitly via `asyncio.Future.set_result(<result>)`.

Eventually, we had our main block, where we created our `asyncio.Future` object and in line `loop = asyncio.get_event_loop()`, we created an instance of the event loop from `asyncio` to execute our coroutine, as shown in the following code:

```
if __name__ == '__main__':
    future = asyncio.Future()
    loop = asyncio.get_event_loop()
    loop.run_until_complete(sleep_coroutine(future))
```

 Tasks and coroutines only execute when the event loop is in execution.

In the final line, `loop.run_until_complete(sleep_coroutine(future))`, we ask our event loop to run until our coroutine has finished its execution. This is done through the `BaseEventLoop.run_until_complete` method presented in the `BaseEventLoop` class.

 The magic to resume a coroutine in `asyncio` is in the `set_result` method of `asyncio.Future` object. All the coroutines to be resumed need to wait for `asyncio.Future` to execute the `set_result` method. So, the event loop of `asyncio` will know that computing has ended and it can resume the coroutine.

Using asyncio.Task

As mentioned before, the `asyncio.Task` class is a subclass of `asyncio.Future` and aims at managing a coroutine. Let us check an example code named `asyncio_task_sample.py`, where more than one object of `asyncio.Task` will be created and dispatched for execution in an event loop of `asyncio`:

```python
import asyncio

@asyncio.coroutine
def sleep_coro(name, seconds=1):
    print("[%s] coroutine will sleep for %d second(s)..."
          % (name, seconds))
    yield yfrom asyncio.sleep(seconds)
    print("[%s] done!" % name)
```

Our coroutine, called `sleep_coro`, will receive two arguments: `name`, which will function as an identifier of our coroutine, and `seconds` with standard value 1, which will indicate for how many seconds the coroutine will be suspended.

Moving on to the main block, we defined a list containing three objects of type `asyncio.Task` named `Task-A`, which will sleep for 10 seconds, and `Task-B` and `Task-C`, which will sleep for 1 second each. See the following code:

```python
if __name__ == '__main__':
    tasks = [asyncio.Task(sleep_coro('Task-A', 10)),
             asyncio.Task(sleep_coro('Task-B')),
             asyncio.Task(sleep_coro('Task-C'))]
    loop.run_until_complete(asyncio.gather(*tasks))
```

Still in the main block, we define our event loop making use of the `BaseEventLoop.run_until_complete` function; however, this one receives no more than one coroutine as argument, but a call to `asyncio.gather` (refer to `https://docs.python.org/3.4/library/asyncio-task.html#task-functions` for more information), which is the function that returns as future attaching the results of the list of coroutines or futures received as arguments. The output of the `asyncio_task_sample.py` program is shown in the following screenshot:

```
yipman@foshan:~/Documents/packpub_chapter08_codes$ python3.4 asyncio_task_sample.py
[Task-A] coroutine will sleep for 10 second(s)...
[Task-B] coroutine will sleep for 1 second(s)...
[Task-C] coroutine will sleep for 1 second(s)...
[Task-B] done!
[Task-C] done!
[Task-A] done!
yipman@foshan:~/Documents/packpub_chapter08_codes$
```

asyncio_task_sample.py output

It is noticeable that the output of the program presents the tasks being performed in the order they are declared; however, none of them can block the event loop. This is due to the fact that Task-B and Task-C sleep less and end before Task-A that sleeps 10 times more and is dispatched first. A scene where Task-A blocks an event loop is catastrophic.

Using an incompatible library with asyncio

The asyncio module is still recent within the Python community. Some libraries are still not fully compatible. Let us refactor our previous section example asyncio_task_sample.py and alter the function from asyncio.sleep to time. sleep in the time module that does not return as a future and check its behavior. We altered the yield from asyncio.sleep(seconds) line to yield from time. sleep(seconds).We obviously need to import the time module to make use of the new sleep. Running the example, notice the new behavior in the output shown in the following screenshot:

```
yipman@foshan:~/Documents/packpub_chapter08_codes$ python3.4 asyncio_task_sample.py
[Task-A] coroutine will sleep for 10 second(s)...
[Task-B] coroutine will sleep for 1 second(s)...
[Task-C] coroutine will sleep for 1 second(s)...
Traceback (most recent call last):
  File "asyncio_task_sample.py", line 19, in <module>
    loop.run_until_complete(asyncio.gather(*tasks))
  File "/usr/lib/python3.4/asyncio/base_events.py", line 208, in run_until_complete
    return future.result()
  File "/usr/lib/python3.4/asyncio/futures.py", line 243, in result
    raise self._exception
  File "/usr/lib/python3.4/asyncio/tasks.py", line 302, in _step
    result = next(coro)
  File "asyncio_task_sample.py", line 9, in sleep_coro
    yield from time.sleep(sleep_seconds)
TypeError: 'NoneType' object is not iterable
yipman@foshan:~/Documents/packpub_chapter08_codes$ 
```

asyncio_task_sample.py output using time.sleep

We can notice that the coroutines are initialized normally, but an error occurs as the yield from syntax waits for a coroutine or asyncio.Future, and time.sleep does not generate anything at its end. So, how should we proceed in these cases? The answer is easy; we need an asyncio.Future object, and then we refactor our example.

First, let us create a function that will create an `asyncio.Future` object to return it to `yield from` present in the `sleep_coro` coroutine. The `sleep_func` function is as follows:

```
def sleep_func(seconds):
    f = asyncio.Future()
    time.sleep(seconds)
    f.set_result("Future done!")
    return f
```

Notice that the `sleep_func` function, as it ends, executes `f.set_result("Future done!")` placing a dummy result in future cause as this computing does not generate a concrete result; it is only a sleep function. Then, an `asyncio.Future` object is returned, which is expected by `yield from` to resume the `sleep_coro` coroutine. The following screenshot illustrates the output of the modified `asyncio_task_sample.py` program:

```
yipman@foshan:~/Documents/packpub_chapter08_codes$ python3.4 asyncio_task_sample.py
[Task-A] coroutine will sleep for 10 second(s)...
[Task-A] done!
[Task-B] coroutine will sleep for 1 second(s)...
[Task-B] done!
[Task-C] coroutine will sleep for 1 second(s)...
[Task-C] done!
yipman@foshan:~/Documents/packpub_chapter08_codes$
```

asyncio_task_sample.py with time.sleep

Now all the dispatched tasks execute without errors. But, wait! There is still something wrong with the output shown in the previous screenshot. Notice that the sequence of execution has something weird within, as `Task-A` sleeps for 10 seconds and ends before the beginning of the two following tasks that sleep only for 1 second. That is, our event loop is being blocked by the tasks. This is a consequence of using a library or module that does not work asynchronously with `asyncio`.

A way to solve this problem is delegating a blocking task to `ThreadPoolExecutor` (remember this works well if the processing is I/O bound; if it is CPU-bound, use `ProcessPoolExecutor`. For our comfort, `asyncio` supports this mechanism in a very simple way. Let us again refactor our `asyncio_task_sample.py` code in order to provide execution to the tasks without blocking the event loop.

Firstly, we must remove the `sleep_func` function as it is no longer necessary. A call to `time.sleep` will be done by the `BaseEventLoop.run_in_executor` method. Let's then refactor our `sleep_coro` coroutine in the following way:

```
@asyncio.coroutine
def sleep_coro(name, loop, seconds=1):
    future = loop.run_in_executor(None, time.sleep, seconds)
```

```
print("[%s] coroutine will sleep for %d second(s)…" %
    (name, seconds))
yield from future
print("[%s] done!" % name)
```

It is noticeable that the coroutine receives a new argument that will be the event loop we created in the main block so that ThreadPoolExecutor is used to respond to the same with the results of executions.

After that, we have the following line:

```
future = loop.run_in_executor(None, time.sleep, seconds)
```

In the previous line, a call to the BaseEventLoop.run_in_executor function was made, and the first argument for it was an executor (https://docs.python. org/3.4/library/concurrent.futures.html#concurrent.futures.Executor). If it passes None, it will use ThreadPoolExecutor as default. The second argument is a callback function, in this case, the time.sleep function that represents our computing to be accomplished, and finally we can pass the callback arguments.

Notice that the BaseEventLoop.run_in_executor method returns an asyncio. Future object. However, it is enough to make a call yield from passing the returned future, and our coroutine is ready.

Remember, we need to alter the main block of the program, passing the event loop to sleep_coro:

```
if__name__ == '__main__':
    loop = asyncio.get_event_loop()

    tasks = [asyncio.Task(sleep_coro('Task-A', loop, 10)),
              asyncio.Task(sleep_coro('Task-B', loop)),
              asyncio.Task(sleep_coro('Task-C', loop))]

    loop.run_until_complete(asyncio.gather(*tasks))
    loop.close()
```

Let us see the refactored code execution shown in the following screenshot:

```
yipman@foshan:~/Documents/packpub_chapter08_codes$ python3.4 asyncio_task_sample.py
[Task-A] coroutine will sleep for 10 second(s)...
[Task-B] coroutine will sleep for 1 second(s)...
[Task-C] coroutine will sleep for 1 second(s)...
[Task-B] done!
[Task-C] done!
[Task-A] done!
yipman@foshan:~/Documents/packpub_chapter08_codes$ ▏
```

We got it! The result is consistent, and the event loop is not blocked by the execution of the `time.sleep` function.

Summary

In this chapter, we have learned about asynchronous, blocking, and nonblocking programming. We have made use of some basic mechanisms of `asyncio` in order to see the nuts and bolts of this mechanism's behavior in some situations.

The `asyncio` module is an attempt to reboot the support to asynchronous programming in Python. Guido Van Rossum was extremely successful in exploring alternatives and thinking of something that could be used as a basis to these alternatives offering a clear API. The `yield from` syntax was born to enhance the expressivity of some programs that use coroutines, relieving the burden on the developer of writing callbacks to treat the ending of events, although it is possible to use callbacks. The `asyncio` module, beyond other advantages, has the capacity of integrating with other applications, as in the Tornado web server, for instance, that already has a support branch to event loop in `asyncio`.

We come to the end of this book, which was indeed challenging to write, and I hope this content can be useful for you. Some tools were left out, such as IPython, mpi4py, Greenlets, Eventlets, and others.

Based on the content offered in this book, you can conduct your own analysis and tests between the examples presented along the different chapters to compare the different tools. The fact in relation to using two main examples along most chapters, was intended to demonstrate that Python allows us to easily change the tools used to solve a problem without changing the core of the solution.

We have learned a bit of **Global Interpreter Lock** (**GIL**) and some workarounds to skip GIL's side effects. It is believed that the main Python implementation (CPython) won't solve the questions related to GIL; only the future can reveal that. GIL is a difficult and recurrent topic in the Python community. On the other hand, we have the PyPy implementation, which brought JIT and other performance improvements along. Nowadays, the PyPy team is working on experimental uses of **Software Transactional Memory** (**STM**) into PyPy, aiming to remove GIL.

Index

Thank you for buying
Parallel Programming with Python

About Packt Publishing

Packt, pronounced 'packed', published its first book "*Mastering phpMyAdmin for Effective MySQL Management*" in April 2004 and subsequently continued to specialize in publishing highly focused books on specific technologies and solutions.

Our books and publications share the experiences of your fellow IT professionals in adapting and customizing today's systems, applications, and frameworks. Our solution based books give you the knowledge and power to customize the software and technologies you're using to get the job done. Packt books are more specific and less general than the IT books you have seen in the past. Our unique business model allows us to bring you more focused information, giving you more of what you need to know, and less of what you don't.

Packt is a modern, yet unique publishing company, which focuses on producing quality, cutting-edge books for communities of developers, administrators, and newbies alike. For more information, please visit our website: www.packtpub.com.

About Packt Open Source

In 2010, Packt launched two new brands, Packt Open Source and Packt Enterprise, in order to continue its focus on specialization. This book is part of the Packt Open Source brand, home to books published on software built around Open Source licenses, and offering information to anybody from advanced developers to budding web designers. The Open Source brand also runs Packt's Open Source Royalty Scheme, by which Packt gives a royalty to each Open Source project about whose software a book is sold.

Writing for Packt

We welcome all inquiries from people who are interested in authoring. Book proposals should be sent to author@packtpub.com. If your book idea is still at an early stage and you would like to discuss it first before writing a formal book proposal, contact us; one of our commissioning editors will get in touch with you.

We're not just looking for published authors; if you have strong technical skills but no writing experience, our experienced editors can help you develop a writing career, or simply get some additional reward for your expertise.

Python High Performance Programming

ISBN: 978-1-78328-845-8   Paperback: 108 pages

Boost the performance of your Python programs using advanced techniques

1. Identify the bottlenecks in your applications and solve them using the best profiling techniques.

2. Write efficient numerical code in NumPy and Cython.

3. Adapt your programs to run on multiple processors with parallel programming.

OpenCL Parallel Programming Development Cookbook

ISBN: 978-1-84969-452-0   Paperback: 302 pages

Accelerate your applications and understand high-performance computing with over 50 OpenCL recipes

1. Learn about parallel programming development in OpenCL and also the various techniques involved in writing high-performing code.

2. Find out more about data-parallel or task-parallel development and also about the combination of both.

3. Understand and exploit the underlying hardware features like processor registers and caches that run potentially tens of thousands of threads across the processors.

Please check **www.PacktPub.com** for information on our titles

Python Network Programming Cookbook

ISBN: 978-1-84951-346-3   Paperback: 234 pages

Over 70 detailed recipes to develop practical solutions for a wide range of real-world network programming tasks

1. Demonstrates how to write various besopke client/server networking applications using standard and popular third-party Python libraries.

2. Learn how to develop client programs for networking protocols such as HTTP/HTTPS, SMTP, POP3, FTP, CGI, XML-RPC, SOAP, and REST.

Instant Parallel Processing with Gearman

ISBN: 978-1-78328-407-8   Paperback: 58 pages

Learn how to use Gearman to build scalable distributed application

1. Learn something new in an Instant! A short, fast, focused guide delivering immediate results.

2. Build a cluster of managers, workers, and clients using Gearman to scale your application.

3. Understand how to reduce single-points-of-failure in your distributed applications.

4. Build clients and workers to process data in the background and provide real-time updates to your frontend.

Please check **www.PacktPub.com** for information on our titles